The Tragedy of Julius Caesar

The Shakespeare Workbook Series

The Tragedy of Julius Caesar

The Shakespeare Workbook Series

Commentary by
John Russell Brown and Neil Freeman

Edited by Paul Sugarman

BLOOMSBURY ACADEMIC
NEW YORK • LONDON • OXFORD • NEW DELHI • SYDNEY

BLOOMSBURY ACADEMIC

Bloomsbury Publishing Inc, 1359 Broadway, 12th Floor, New York, NY 10018, USA
Bloomsbury Publishing Plc, 50 Bedford Square, London, WC1B 3DP, UK
Bloomsbury Publishing Ireland, 29 Earlsfort Terrace, Dublin 2, D02 AY28, Ireland

BLOOMSBURY, BLOOMSBURY ACADEMIC and the Diana logo are trademarks of Bloomsbury Publishing Plc

First published in the United States of America 2026

Copyright © Bloomsbury Publishing, 2026

Material drawn from *Shakescenes: Shakespeare for Two*
Copyright © 1992 Applause Theatre Book Publishers

Material drawn from *Once More Unto the Speech, Dear Friends*
Copyright © 2006 Folio Scripts, Vancouver, Canada

Material drawn from *The Tragedy of Julius Caesar: The Applause Shakespeare Library*
Copyright © 1996 Applause Books

Introduction and other additional material © 2026 Paul Sugarman

Cover design: Chloe Batch

All rights reserved. No part of this publication may be: i) reproduced or transmitted in any form, electronic or mechanical, including photocopying, recording or by means of any information storage or retrieval system without prior permission in writing from the publishers; or ii) used or reproduced in any way for the training, development or operation of artificial intelligence (AI) technologies, including generative AI technologies. The rights holders expressly reserve this publication from the text and data mining exception as per Article 4(3) of the Digital Single Market Directive (EU) 2019/790.

Bloomsbury Publishing Inc does not have any control over, or responsibility for, any third-party websites referred to or in this book. All internet addresses given in this book were correct at the time of going to press. The author and publisher regret any inconvenience caused if addresses have changed or sites have ceased to exist, but can accept no responsibility for any such changes.

Library of Congress Cataloging-in-Publication Data Available

ISBN: PB: 978-1-4930-5702-3
ePDF: 979-8-7651-5805-0
eBook: 978-1-4930-5703-0

Typeset by Amnet

For product safety related questions contact productsafety@bloomsbury.com.
To find out more about our authors and books visit www.bloomsbury.com and sign up for our newsletters.

CONTENTS

Introduction by Paul Sugarman 7

Original Practices and Cue Scripts by Paul Sugarman 11

Advice to Actors by John Russell Brown 14

Brief Background to the First Folio by Neil Freeman 31

Scene Study: Act IV, Scene iii (Cassius and Brutus) 42

Working on Modern and First Folio Texts

    Act I, Scene ii (Brutus, Cassius) 56

    Act II, Scene i (Brutus) 68

    Act II, Scene i (Brutus, Portia) 72

    Act III, Scene ii (Antony) 82

OVERVIEW: WORKING ON SHAKESPEARE TO BUILD TOWARD PERFORMANCE

Perform the Text: Share the text with a wider audience.

Share the Text: Speak the text to someone else.

Action: Find the Choices in the Text: What choices can be made in terms of the character?

Explore the Text: Consult the First Folio to see how capitalization, punctuation, and line endings can shift emphasis. Connect to the text physically and personally.

Analyze the Text: Look at the text in depth to see how it works. Is it verse or prose?

Understand the Text: You need to understand what is being said and what all the words mean.

Read the Text Aloud: These words were meant to be spoken.

INTRODUCTION

Paul Sugarman

The aim of this Applause Shakespeare Workbook is to provide tools for working on the text of *The Tragedy of Julius Caesar*. Out of the many Bloomsbury publications on Shakespeare this book draws material from the works of John Russell Brown (*Shakescenes* and the Applause Shakespeare Library) and Neil Freeman (*Once More Unto the Speech* series and the Folio Texts) to give you and/or your actors or students practical approaches to work on the text.

These plays, while they speak much to our human condition today, are from more than four hundred years ago. To fully appreciate Shakespeare, there is a lot that one needs to know. There are many books published by Bloomsbury that can help you understand and work on Shakespeare. First you need to understand the time when he lived, which has similarities to today and many differences. *William Shakespeare: A Popular Life* by Garry O'Connor gives insight into Shakespeare's time. Much like Stephen Greenblatt's *Will in the World*, it paints a picture of Shakespeare's age and makes connections between that time and the text in his plays that give a broader perspective on the images and references in Shakespeare's works.

There is the need for much more in-depth study and work on how to use your voice to speak the text. Bloomsbury publishes *The Actor and the Text* by Cicely Berry, which reveals how Shakespeare uses language to express so much in such a wide variety of ways and the need to have a strong and connected voice to be able to do it justice. She includes hands-on approaches to the text to show how Shakespeare uses rhetoric to make his points. Her *Working Shakespeare* video series shows many top UK and US actors putting her techniques into practice.

There is also the practicality of how to understand his work in performance. One of John Russell Brown's central ideas is that you can't fully understand and appreciate Shakespeare without understanding how it works in performance. He wrote many books on Shakespeare and many editions of the works of Shakespeare and other early modern playwrights. Bloomsbury publishes many of his books including

Shakescenes, which provides material for this book; and *Shakespeare's Plays in Performance*, which looks at performance elements and performance history. *Free Shakespeare* contrasts how the plays were originally performed with the vision of the actor-based ensembles, which has been influential for many American acting companies. John Russell Brown created the Applause Shakespeare Library, which included theatrical commentary to make sure that performance considerations are an essential part of studying the play. There is also much that can be gained from great performers of Shakespeare as shown by John Gielgud's books *Acting Shakespeare* and *An Actor and His Time*, as well as the many fine biographies of great stage actors such as Gielgud, Laurence Olivier, and Ralph Richardson, also published by Bloomsbury.

The importance of the first collected publication of Shakespeare's plays, the First Folio of 1623, cannot be underestimated. It collected thirty-six of Shakespeare's plays, eighteen of which had never been published before and would have been lost forever. Bloomsbury publishes all thirty-six plays from the First Folio in individual editions that were prepared and annotated by Neil Freeman. Bloomsbury publishes the single volume *The Applause First Folio of Shakespeare in Modern Type*. Freeman then went on to create the *Once More Unto the Speech* series of books comparing modern and Folio texts for more than nine hundred speeches, demonstrating the practicality of using Folio texts. Material from that series has been made more accessible in the recent series of *Monologues from Shakespeare's First Folio* series of twelve books. Neil Freeman was one of the major forces in making the First Folio more useful for actors and students of the plays.

Both John Russell Brown and Neil Freeman were champions for understanding Shakespeare through performance. John Russell Brown's Applause Shakespeare Library was designed to make one aware of the many opportunities presented by the text for performance. Neil Freeman's First Folio texts showed the many clues and choices that could be explored through looking at the text as originally printed. By taking examples from both men's work, these materials present different perspectives on the text.

The wonderful thing about working on Shakespeare is that there is no one "right" answer. His work endures because it is so flexible and subject to varied interpretations. In your own exploration of the text you have to find which choices work best for you (and, perhaps, your students). To find the best choice you need to explore what is out there and why these more than four-hundred-year-old texts still speak to us today.

This workbook presents a brief description of various approaches to the text by John Russell Brown and Neil Freeman. Following are scenes from the play that John Russell Brown had included in *Shakescenes* along with further selections from the Applause Shakespeare Library edition of the play. Speeches from the play drawn from Neil Freeman's *Once More Unto the Speech* series will give a First Folio perspective on the text.

The goal is to be able to speak and share Shakespeare's words in a way that makes the plays come alive in ways they do not when read silently. Perhaps the biggest perceived challenge is understanding and getting comfortable with Shakespeare's language. Though the language may seem old to us, the English language of Shakespeare was four hundred years *younger* then than it is now, as Kristin Linklater, author of *Freeing Shakespeare's Voice*, observed. Although these words are from four centuries ago, it is still Modern English but in its infancy, when it was still blossoming and expanding. The spoken word was essential to almost all communication in Shakespeare's day, unlike our predominantly visual and text-based age. We don't talk as much or as precisely as those whose lives depended on spoken communication in Shakespeare's time. Shakespeare does a lot more with language than we do in our modern world. Working on Shakespeare's language can open one up to new and more effective ways of communicating. These great thoughts and words show the possibilities of expression that a human voice can achieve.

Basic Steps to Working on Shakespeare's Text

Read the Text Aloud: These words were meant to be spoken. Music cannot be experienced solely by looking at annotations on a page. Neither can Shakespeare.

Understand the Text: You need to understand what is being said and what all the words mean. It is important to consult glossaries that give Elizabethan definitions and context. David and Ben Crystal's website shakespeareswords.com is a good place to start.

Analyze the Text: Look at the text in depth to see how it works. Is it verse or prose? If verse, where is it regular and where not? Shakespeare uses rhetorical devices to convey feelings and meanings. How do the sounds and words "play" off each other?

Explore the Text: Consult the First Folio to see how capitalization, punctuation, and line endings can shift emphasis. Connect to the text physically and personally. How do the words and sounds feel inside your body?

Action: Find the Choices in the Text: What choices can be made in terms of the character? What actions can they take? What choices can be made about their needs? Some choices may seem obvious, but look for the possibilities of different ones.

Share the Text: Speak the text to someone else so that you can assess how well you are communicating the thoughts beneath the text.

Perform the Text: Share the text with a wider audience, to whom you can also speak directly, as there was no fourth wall in Shakespeare's theater.

Committing to speaking Shakespeare's text requires more of us than most contemporary communication does. Energize the whole body when giving voice to the text. There have been many fine books on using the voice to support Shakespeare text work including *The Actor and the Text* by Cicely Berry (Applause) and *Freeing Shakespeare's Voice* by Kristin Linklater (TCG).

The exploration of the text can continue indefinitely as there is no one answer to these texts but an endless array of possibilities to be explored. However, if you start with speaking and listening instead of just reading the words, it will lead you to a more personal connection to the text.

Shakespeare connects to so many people in different ways because we find something in our personal lives that is explained by the way Shakespeare says it. Sometimes the text instantly makes sense to you, but often the possibilities are infinite. We make choices based on how the text connects to us at this moment in our time.

This workbook will outline some of the tools to look at the text and give examples from the works of John Russell Brown and Neil Freeman, who can offer differing viewpoints on the same text as a way for you to learn to trust your ear and your connection to the text. This workbook will show ways to work on the text with a spirit of exploration.

ORIGINAL PRACTICES AND CUE SCRIPTS

Paul Sugarman

What do we know of the original practices of Shakespeare's time? Most of the evidence we have comes from Philip Henslowe, who was the owner of the Rose Theatre. His "diary," which was a log book of receipts for shows that they would perform 6 days a week, including many different plays. In a month where they could do 24–27 performances they would stage 15–20 different plays with only a few repeated more than once. We have little documentation on the rehearsal and performance practices of the time, but we are able to get an idea of how they worked from references in plays (such as the Mechanicals rehearsals in *A Midsummer Night's Dream*) and the papers left by Edward Alleyn, Henslowe's son-in-law and the lead actor of The Lord Admiral's Men.

Edward Alleyn was, along with Richard Burbage, one of the leading actors of Shakespeare's time. Alleyn founded Dulwich College, to which he bequeathed papers from his theatrical career, including Henslowe's diary, a cue script from *Orlando Furioso* and a platt (scene plot) for *The Seven Deadlie Sinnes* from which scholars have deduced what we know of the rehearsal practices of the day. Instead of receiving the full text, the actors would get a cue script which had their lines and the line that came before their line (their cue). A platt was a listing of all the scenes with entrances and sound cues that would be hung backstage for the cast to refer to.

The cue scripts were hand-written by copyists. By just giving the actors their lines and cues it was easier for the company than providing a whole script. Also, it allowed the company to maintain tighter control over the complete text of a play since copyright didn't really exist back then. If a rival company of actors got hold of a play text there would be nothing to stop them from performing it. Full scripts were kept under lock and key at the theatre.

Cue scripts have enjoyed something of a renaissance with Patrick Tucker (another contemporary champion of the First Folio). The Original Shakespeare Company created by Tucker did performances using scrolls with very minimal rehearsal to mimic the conditions under which the plays might usually have been done.

A number of Shakespeare companies work with cue scripts. Cue script Shakespeare performances have been presented by many companies that did readings from scrolls, including the Actors Shakespeare Company and Spontaneous Shakespeare. For readings they are quite useful as they are compact enough that one can move easily with them and it can look more like a performance than a reading in which actors are carrying around conspicuous scripts.

They are very useful for learning lines, as you can focus solely on your cues, dialogue, and speeches. They are convenient to carry around. There are a number of actors who have told me that they set up cue scripts when they're doing contemporary plays as well, as they are just a useful mechanism for learning lines. In Shakespeare's time, scrolls were also referred to as "rolls," and it is possible that the term "roles" came from this usage.

How to Make Your Own Scrolls

One can make up one's own scrolls for parts with an electronic version of the text.

The materials needed are quite readily available except for the dowels which form their basis. I have seen people make scrolls of unsharpened pencils, but those are too short and thin for an effective scroll base. You need two ½-inch dowels 8–9-inches long, paper, scissors, scotch tape, and covered hair elastics. (Dowel rods come in varying lengths; you can get several scrolls from one rod.)

Of course, once you make a digital cue script you can read it on your phone or mobile device. However, I find that having a physical scroll leads to quicker memorization.

Starting with the digital file for the script, using Word or similar software, just cut out everyone else's lines except for their cues for your character's lines. A cue wouldn't be the full prior speech but just the last 3–5 words of their speech.

The text should be formatted so that it is in a large enough font to be easily readable and formatted so that it is no wider than 5-inches wide.

Print out your scroll, trim the paper so that it is about 6–6½ inches wide, and tape it to one of the dowels. As you trim the pages, tape them together so that they flow continuously. While you add to your role you can roll what you have done on to the dowel and secure it with a binder clip to keep it from unrolling. When you get to the end of the end of your role, you tape it to the other dowel.

Then you use the hair rubber bands to hold the dowels together and move back and forth in the part. As you become comfortable you can easily advance the scroll with one hand.

ADVICE TO ACTORS

John Russell Brown

There is no such person as a "Shakespearean actor," if that phrase implies the possession of unique qualifications or unusual gifts. Shakespeare's plays are available to all good actors, no matter what their training or experience may be.

Yet, of course, the texts reprinted here are not like those of modern plays. Shakespeare does present special problems, and the blunt assurance that his writing is open for anyone to explore will not sound very convincing to a student-actor meeting it for the first time. The following approaches are offered as encouragement to make a start and free imagination to work intelligently on the texts.

Character

First of all, an actor in any play must discover the person behind the words of any particular role. Of course, an actor must learn how to speak the character's lines clearly and forcefully, but that alone will not bring the play to life. Speech is not all, because Shakespeare did not write for talking heads. He first imagined individual persons in lively interplay with each other and *then* conjured words for them to speak; and that is the best sequence for an actor to follow. A living person has to be brought to the stage, and then he can begin to speak and become realized in the process.

In Elizabethan times, plays were performed on a large platform stage that jutted out into the middle of a crowded audience, many of whom were standing rather than sitting as is the custom today; and in this open arena everything took place by daylight. Some performances were given indoors, but then the audience was illuminated along with the actors. Such conditions were more like those of a public meeting in our day, or of a booth in a fairground. They called for an acting style that was grounded in a basic physical delineation of each character. An actor had to maintain the vibrant outlines of the role so that his performance could be viewed from all sides and at all times whenever he was on stage.

Character Questions

BASIC QUESTIONS:

- How does the character move and speak?
- How think and feel?
- Where does this individual come from? What does he know? What does he want?
- What does he look like, sound like?
- How could anyone recognize the person who speaks these lines?
- Why does this particular person need to speak these particular words?
- How old is this person?
- What physical characteristics are essential for an impersonation?
- What is this person's family situation?
- What are the political, professional, and social conditions of his life?

MORE DIFFICULT QUESTIONS FOLLOW, WHICH HELP TO DEFINE PERSONALITY AND CONSCIOUSNESS:

- How does this person "see" and respond to the world around him?
- What does he like and dislike? What does he pursue and what does he seek to avoid?
- What conventions, social pressures, or political forces influence behavior, either consciously or unconsciously?

INTERROGATING THE TEXT:

- What verbs does the character use?
- How does he talk to other characters?
- Do questions, assertions, explanations, answers, excuses, qualifications, elaborations, or repetitions predominate?
- Are sentences long or short, leisured and assured, or compact and urgent?
- Are sentences governed by a single main verb?

- Or are they supplied with a sequence of phrases, each governed by its own subsidiary verb?
- How does this person refer to others: always in the same way, or with variations? With different names, titles, or endearments?
- Is address intimate or formal, simple or elaborate?
- Or is contact between two characters assumed and assured, so that names are not required at all?

Normally such detailed verbal enquiry is a continuous process that goes on throughout a long rehearsal period. Scrutiny of every word in even a short scene will help to develop a sensitivity to words, a facility that can be drawn upon constantly throughout an actor's career in whatever plays he may perform.

ALL KINDS OF EXERCISES CAN HELP:

- Very slow rehearsals encourage full awareness of what is thought and felt, as the words are spoken easily without thought of projecting or shaping them.
- Silent rehearsals, with someone else speaking the text.
- Improvised explorations of moments of encounter or retreat.
- Improvised paraphrasing of Shakespeare's text.
- Sessions in which the actors sit back-to-back and only speak the words, trying to communicate fully.
- Variations in positions, so that the two actors are at first close and then far apart, quite still and then always on the move, looking at each other or refusing to do so, paying attention to nothing but the sound of words or engaged on other business—all these explorations may find new means of expression or more physical enactments for a scene.
- Questions should be asked, as for any play, to encourage a fuller sense of what is afoot in a scene: What do they expect from each other? How secure or insecure are they?

What we can deduce about Elizabethan stage practice should encourage present-day actors to seek out distinctive physical characteristics for each role they play in Shakespeare, possess or embody them as fully as possible, and then play the text boldly. This will provide the appropriate dynamic and credibility.

The moment actors walk onto the stage in character, they must be strong and expressive, even before a word has been spoken. Then as each person is drawn into the drama, there must be no loss of definition but growth, development, and surprise. As the play continues, new facets and new resources will be revealed, until each character has become fully present and open to an audience. In performance, actors need to be alert and active and must possess great reserves of energy. They are like boxers in a ring who dare not lose concentration or the ability to perform at full power. They have to watch, listen, move, and speak, and at the same time embody the persons they represent. It is like levitating, or flying through the air, by a continuous act of will and imagination. Characters must have clarity; actors, courage.

But how can an actor find the person to present? Trial and error play no small role in shaping a trained instinct for Shakespeare's people. And this trial begins with a close interrogation of the text.

In a search for the person to bring onstage, first impressions may be deceptive or, rather, limiting. For example, on a first reading, Romeo and Juliet may appear to be two "typical" romantic lovers who delight in each other's presence and have much in common, including parents who would disapprove very strongly of their love if they were to know of it. All that is true and useful, but if the two actors for these roles were each to make a list of the nouns in their respective speeches, two very different sensibilities and personalities would be revealed. The minds of Romeo and Juliet run in different directions; they have their own sensations and feelings, and distinct views of the world around them.

There are many constructive ways of studying Shakespeare's words beyond tracing verb patterns. Preparing lists of adjectives and adverbs may reveal when and where a character is sufficiently thoughtful to qualify an idea, although some speakers in some scenes will never have sufficient command or perception to use a qualifying or descriptive word. Lists of double meanings, similes, metaphors, references to other realities than the one on-stage—whether the imagined world is distant, intimate, literary, political, religious, or historical—can help to show the deeper resources of a character's mind.

Slowly, by such analysis of the text, a psychological "identikit" can be assembled, marking predominant colors, preconceptions, modes of thought and feeling. Many such separate and small details begin to suggest a more embracing idea about a person.

On the other hand, it would be a mistake to read and analyze for too long; an actor needs to start to act and to speak just as soon as intuition and imagination are quickened by more deliberate investigations. The actor's own being has to be satisfied and used in performance, as well as the details of the text.

Slowly, a sense of the character's consciousness will emerge, and a number of physical traits will become established. So, the stage character should evolve slowly, from within itself, freshly and uniquely created; actions will suit the words and reveal a sense of being that attracts and repays attention. There is no knowing what may happen. One danger is that too many details will attract attention so that the basic presence is left undeveloped. After making his discoveries, the actor must therefore decide which of his discoveries are truly necessary and which can be discarded.

Careful and patient study, analysis, exploration, imitation, quiet impulse, quick imagination, and the luck of adventurous rehearsal all have a contribution to make in the creation of these plays.

Verse, Prose, and Language

Laurence Olivier in his portrayal of the lead in *Henry the Fifth* decided to be real, rather than phony, grand, or rhetorical. So he "got underneath the lines," and in rehearsal his acting became so close to natural behavior that the words were sometimes indistinct and difficult to hear. Then one day, Tyrone Guthrie, the director, stopped the rehearsal—he had been away for a while and insisted that this actor should perform the verse and the rhetoric: "Larry . . . let's have it properly," he called out from the back of the theater. For a moment, Olivier hesitated and then did as he was told; and the change, as he tells the story, was instantaneous and transforming. He had always known that verse and sentence structure, and imagery, were instructing him to speak with confidence, enjoyment, and resonance, and that they had a commanding and developing power, but he had held back in distrust. Now he found that artificial verse and grand language fitted his character like necessary and proper clothes, and they gave him the ability to rouse his audience on stage and in the auditorium. (When he came to act the part in the film, they even roused his horse.) Olivier was still truthful, but now he was also heroic.

Poetry is the natural idiom of Shakespeare's stage, as swimming is for the ocean, singing for opera or musical theater, controlled and exceptional movement for dance, or solemnity for great occasions. Speaking Shakespeare's verse becomes as instinctive as song, and the actor forgets that he is being metrically correct and vocally subtle.

Elizabethan audiences were so convinced by performances in which verse was spoken that a play written wholly in prose would be more likely to seem artificial. Today Shakespeare's plays can become *just* as real, if actors both use the verse and also act with truth to life. Bernard Shaw advised actors in Shakespeare's early plays to treat the verse like a child does a swing, without self-consciousness or hesitation. In later plays the art of verse is more demanding and the pleasure it gives deeper, but both must be similarly instinctive.

Until verse speaking has become second nature—as it quite quickly does—an actor should study the meter of the lines well in advance of rehearsals, methodically picking out the words to be stressed and finding, by trial and error, the most appropriate phrasing. It is necessary to speak the lines out loud, so that meaning and syntax can be related to the demands of versification and *vice versa*. Breathing and speaking should work together so that the energy of thought and feeling responds to the text and begins to motivate speech. Texture, linked variations of sound, alliteration, assonance, rhyme, and rhythm must all be heeded. These concepts cannot be explored fully in the mind. By speaking the words, their sounds and visceral impact will reveal different levels of meaning. Phrasing, breathing, tempo, pace, pitch, intonation, silence have all to be considered. The lines must be spoken aloud again and again, as one way of speaking is tested against another; and then, slowly, by following the clues inherent in the text, a fully responsive delivery can emerge.

When using this book, start to "do" whenever doubt arises. Generations of actors will assure you that with practice, the acting of Shakespeare's poetry—not merely the speaking of it—becomes instinctive and fluent, pleasurable and, in the context of the play, both true and natural.

The actor should begin by appreciating Shakespeare's preferred medium, the iambic pentameter. Each line should have ten syllables, alternately weak and strong, so that each pair of syllables forms one "foot," and five feet complete a line. Although few pentameters are entirely regular—

if they were, the dialogue would be unbearably wooden and predictable—all follow the ongoing pattern to some degree. It is their likeness that links them together, while their irregularity draws attention to particular words, varies rhythm and pace, and lends a forward movement to speech as disturbance of pattern awakens an expectation that pattern will be reasserted and finally satisfied.

STEPS TO ANALYZING THE TEXT

- Is it verse or prose?
- If verse, is it regular or irregular? Many lines are irregular with stresses not following the iambic pattern or if there are other than ten syllables in a line.
- Speak the text to find the most natural emphasis.

Sense, syntax, speakability, and an underlying regularity are the principal guides in scanning a line, but they do not always provide an unequivocal lead. Until well-practiced in verse speaking, a student should mark the text in pencil, changing the stresses until sure enough to start rehearsals. Still more changes may be made later, before this slow and methodical preparation can be forgotten and taken for granted—that is the last and absolutely necessary part of the process.

Scansion

In deciding how to scan a line, some general rules may be applied. Nouns and verbs always need to be stressed in order to make the sense clear—more stressed than adjectives, adverbs, pronouns, prepositions, or conjunctions. Moreover the fourth syllable of any line, being the most able to reestablish the normal pattern after irregularities and most in control of each individual line, is nearly always stressed in a regular way. If the end of a line is irregular, the beginning of the following one is likely to be regular, for two, or three, consecutive feet. However, the first foot in a line is very frequently irregular, since a reversed foot, with the strong syllable coming first, gives fresh impetus to new thought.

An example from an early play gives clear indication of both regularity and irregularity:

(King Edward speaks to his queen about political enemies.)

⏑ — ⏑ — ⏑ — ⏑ ⏑ — —
My love, forbear to fawn upon their frowns.

⏑ — ⏑ — ⏑ — ⏑ — ⏑ — ⏑
What danger or what sorrow can befall thee

⏑ — ⏑ — ⏑ — ⏑ — ⏑ —
So long as Edward is thy constant friend

⏑ — ⏑ — ⏑ — ⏑ — ⏑ —
And their true sovereign whom they must obey?

— ⏑ ⏑ — ⏑ — ⏑ — — —
Nay, whom they shall obey, and love thee too,   5

⏑ — ⏑ — ⏑ — ⏑ ⏑ — —
Unless they seek for hatred at my hands—

⏑ — ⏑ — — ⏑ ⏑ — ⏑ —
Which if they do, yet will I keep thee safe

⏑ — ⏑ — ⏑ — ⏑ ⏑ — —
And they shall feel the vengeance of my wrath.
(Henry VI, Part iii, IV.i.75–82)

Some of the strong stresses marked in these lines might be changed, but very few; and all its irregularities are brief. The close of line 5 is most problematical: it is marked here with three consecutive strong syllables as the sense of the parenthesis seems to require, but the final "too" might be unstressed or, possibly, the penultimate "thee." (Three consecutive strong stresses should be used very sparingly, because they doubly disturb the underlying norm.) A similar uncertainty arises at the end of line 2, which is marked here with the final "thee" as an extra unstressed syllable. Alternatively, "can" would not be stressed and "befall" counted as a single strong syllable, so that "thee" could follow with equal stress.

All the strong syllables are not equally stressed in speech, and here actors have much more liberty to find the emphasis that suits their own interpretation of a character. Many choices are available. In most iambic pentameters only three syllables take major emphasis, the other stressed syllables being only slightly more prominent than the unstressed ones. So one reading of the same passage might be:

My love, *forbear* to *fawn* upon their *frowns.*
What *danger* or what sorrow can *befall* thee

> So *long* as Edward is thy constant friend
> And their true sovereign whom they *must obey?*
> Nay, whom they *shall* obey, and *love thee* too,
> Unless they *seek* for *hatred* at my *hands*
> Which if they *do,* yet will I *keep* thee *safe*
> And they shall feel the *vengeance* of my *wrath.*

Perhaps the first line should have four major emphases, as Edward presses his argument. In line 3, "constant" may be more significant than "long" and so take the emphasis; but the "f" in *friend* makes that word able to gain strength from the other stressed *f*s in the preceding lines. Choice of stress will also be influenced by words set either in opposition to contrast with each other or in agreement to reinforce each other. Stressing these words can often clarify the logic of what the speaker is saying. For example, in line 4, "their" might be stressed and the penultimate foot reversed, so that "they" is stressed as well for reinforcement, and "must" would count only as a weak syllable. Such a reading would raise the possibility that in line 7, "thee" might be stressed rather than "keep," so that the "they" in line 8 could be a fourth major emphasis in contrast with "thee," to bring a relatively sturdy finish to the whole speech. But, in general, pronouns should not be emphasized, because that takes away prominence from the nouns and verbs, which have to sustain the sense of any speech; those are the elements that form the supporting backbone for strong dialogue and provide its thought-action and forward impetus.

This simple speech of eight lines illustrates how metrical considerations become, very quickly and necessarily, issues of character as well. The same is true when problems of phrasing are introduced. In the early verse plays especially, a brief pause at the end of each line is usual and provides a further guide to phrasing beyond those inherent in sense and syntax. Yet this is not a constant rule, and sometimes only the slightest rise of pitch or marking of a final consonant is sufficient indication of a line-ending; in this way, two consecutive lines will run into each other almost without hesitation or change of impression. In this passage, if Edward pauses slightly after "friend," the last word of line 3, and after "safe" at the end of line 8, his thoughts of "love" will seem more urgent than those concerning political power because, in this reading, the latter will seem to be afterthoughts. But if line 3 runs over into line 4, without the customary pause at the line-ending, the two reactions become almost inseparable; and then the political motivation will outweigh the amorous, because it is expressed in a longer phrase and placed in a climactic position. The relationship between lines 7 and 8 raises similar possibilities.

A pause, or caesura, may also be marked in mid-line. Syntax or sense will sometimes require this to be done (as in line 7 above), but here too a choice is often to be made. The advantage of a mid-line break is that it can give a sense of ongoing thought and quick intelligence. Some critics would argue that every line should have its caesura, but there is good reason not to supply them too strongly or too consistently; such readings encourage a halting delivery and an impression of weakness, and are not always easy to comprehend. In this passage, the final line would clearly be stronger if there were no hint of a pause in mid-line. So might line 2—unless two slight pauses were given, as if commas had been placed after both "danger" and "sorrow," thus giving Edward a very thoughtful and determined manner of speech. Line 6 also seems to run without a break, unless it came after "seek," so giving point to Edward's personal involvement. Seldom should a mid-line pause be placed so that it breaks up a regular iambic foot; normally it should follow, and therefore still further emphasize, a strong syllable. If a caesura is marked in each line of this passage, a general impression of energetic thought might be given, and in some performances this could be useful.

No decision is solely a technical matter; versification in Shakespeare's mind was an instrument for enhancing a representation of individual characters in lively interplay. Problems of verse-speaking are truly dramatic problems, and so each actor must find solutions that suit his or her own impersonation. Although there are many ways of speaking verse that are clearly wrong—too many stressed syllables one after another is a common fault, and too few clear stresses another—there is no one correct way to speak any speech. A respect for versification offers many opportunities to strengthen one's grasp of the play in action and deepen the rendering of a character's very being.

As in any lifelike dialogue in prose, the actor must ask why speak at all; that is, he must discover and follow the action of thought and feeling beneath the words, sustaining and shaping them. In other terms, syntax is, in the last analysis, more important than meter. Each complete sentence is a distinct action, requiring breath, physical response, and speech, according to its own impulses.

In prose dialogue, sentence structure is the principal means whereby Shakespeare controls and so strengthens an actor's speaking of his text. Often the formal arrangement is very elaborate and sustained. Moreover, its effect is reinforced by the use of a series of parallel phrases and by wordplay; these both hold the subsections together and provide a sense of growth and climax. Exploring how the words play off each other in these ways can reveal the character's intentions. Stressing key words, puns, and affirmations is not enough; the flow and energy of the language have to be represented in performance, giving a sense of exploration, energy, struggle, attainment, frustration. Sentence structure and wordplay define this music and this drama, and the actor must respond to both and transmit both through performance.

Each actor must make his own distinctive response to the challenge of the text. No teacher or director can provide ready-made and sufficient solutions here, and this realization may help to understand something fundamental about the acting of Shakespeare: no instruction can take responsibility away from the actors. Sometimes students are recommended to speak Shakespeare's lines with a certain quality or tone of voice, or a certain accent, and for some exercises or some productions this may be useful. But following such a prescription is likely to do more harm than good, because the actor is distracted from the primary task of finding a voice and being for each character and then responding to the text in his or her own manner. Of course, efficient breathing and voice production are needed to respond to so demanding a text, but technical expertise must always be at the service of the specific demands of character, situation, and speech, as these are discovered by each individual actor.

Some words and phrases in the plays seem to cry out for a great deal of preparatory work, but it may be only a small exaggeration to say that every word, phrase, sentence, and speech may repay in some measure a similar investment. An actor can have an endless adventure when acting Shakespeare, as step by step he gets closer to a fully responsive, individual, and necessary (and therefore convincing) way of turning text into performance.

An actor's mind and body need to be more than usually alert and energized to answer the challenge. What starts as patient and complicated exploration can end, however, in a marvelous extension of an actor's powers of thought, feeling, and being, as the poetry comes to fresh and brilliant life. That is why Shakespeare's plays are so rewarding to perform. By making each word sound as if it is necessary to his or her character, an actor will claim attention with amazing ease.

Toward Performance

All kinds of exercises can help inexperienced actors. Very slow rehearsals encourage full awareness of what is thought and felt, as the words are spoken easily without thought of projecting or shaping them. Silent rehearsals, with someone else speaking the text, improvised explorations of moments of encounter or retreat, improvised paraphrasing of Shakespeare's text, or sessions in which the actors sit back-to-back and only speak the words, trying to communicate fully—all these devices may help performers to become more free, adventurous, and true. Variations in positions, so that the two actors are at first close and then far apart, quite still and then always on the move, looking at each other or refusing to do so, paying attention to nothing but the sound of words or engaged on other business—all these explorations may find new means of expression or more physical enactments for a scene. Questions should be asked, as for any play, to encourage a fuller sense of what is afoot in a scene: What do they expect from each other? How secure or insecure are they? Many of these questions were first asked in individual preparation. None of these ordinary ways of working is foreign to Shakespeare's plays.

When performing modern plays, actors have extensive stage directions in the text to guide them: descriptions of activity, unspoken reactions, movements, pauses, silences, and so on. But in Shakespeare's plays there is little of this, and what is printed in modern editions is often the invention of editors and not what Shakespeare wrote. In the versions of scenes printed in this book, stage directions are very scarce and minimal, but the commentary will often point out activity, movement and responses, that *may* be required for acting the text.

Actors must learn to read Shakespeare's stage directions implicit in the dialogue: clues for tempo, rhythm change, breathing, for closeness or distance between the characters, and so on. Very important, because usually unambiguous, is Shakespeare's use of incomplete verse lines to indicate a pause or silence in the middle of speech, or in the interchange between two people. When two characters share a single verse line, each speaking one half of a regular iambic pentameter, the opposite is true; there should be no pause or hesitation here, the dialogue continuing without break and the new speaker responsive to the phrasing, rhythm, and pitch of the person he follows.

So much can be discovered while working together on a text that simplification must become part of the ongoing process. Actors must identify those elements that are truest and most revealing and develop those at the cost of losing others. The essential part of this process is to recognize what is particularly alive and new in the work and take the necessary steps to allow this to grow.

There is a paradox at the heart of what can be said about the task of acting Shakespeare's plays. Imaginatively the performers need to be exceptionally free, and yet the most liberating work will be found by paying strict attention to the minutest details of the text and using them as spurs to invention and exploration. Shakespeare's imagination seems always to be ahead of ours, beckoning us; and so, if the actor is patient and adventurous, he will find within the text whatever suits his or her individual abilities and point of view. The text can be ever new, and even the most experienced actor or playgoer is liable to be amazed at what is achieved for the first time with any new production.

Of course, actors develop particular ways of working, and their interpretations of a number of roles will have much in common, but it is wise to beware of drawing the possibilities of a Shakespeare text down to the level of performance that a particular actor has found to be reliable. Shakespeare's kings are all different from each other, and so are his fools; and each one is liable to have a different life from scene to scene, sometimes even moment by moment. Even such clear distinctions as that between comedy and drama should be treated with reserve: in important ways, there are no comic and no serious roles in Shakespeare. Hamlet or Prince Hal, Romeo or Juliet all need to raise laughter and act the fool, drawing on skills that are sometimes considered to be appropriate to comedy. Lady Macbeth and Macbeth are deeply involved in a terrible action, but their minds move with swiftness and fantasy, so they play with words, very like witty persons in a comedy. In all Shakespeare's roles, villain or hero, lover or fool, an actor must be ready to respond outside conventional limitations.

When Shakespeare's Prince Hamlet tried to instruct the players who arrived in the court of Elsinore, he was concerned with their technique and their attention to the text, but "their special observance," he said, should be with "nature":

> for anything so o'erdone is from the purpose of playing, whose end, both at the first and now, was and is to hold, as 'twere, the mirror up to nature....
> (*Hamlet*, III.ii.1 ff.)

The key phrase, "hold the mirror up to nature," sounds like a generalized instruction: show everyone what they look like, but in context it is precise. Hamlet is in the process of castigating actors' faults and he continues in the same vein:

> O there be players that I have seen play—and heard others praise, and that highly—not to speak it profanely, that, neither having th'accent of Christians, nor the gait of Christian, pagan nor man, have so strutted and bellowed that I have thought some of Nature's journeymen had made men, and not made them well, they imitated humanity so abominably.

The actors have to "make men"; they have to be highly skilled craftspersons, not ordinary workmen ("journeymen"). Characters have to move and speak, and function, as we do: they have been individually crafted and must be alive with individuality. Slowly, skillfully, and adventurously, an actor must build an illusion of a living being, one for whom Shakespeare's text is a necessary extension of existence. Hamlet does not speak for Shakespeare, but in creating this character the dramatist wrote with such freedom, precision, and obvious pleasure that he must have drawn more deeply than usual on his own ideas and reactions. Lacking Shakespeare's advice to the players, Hamlet's is a good substitute.

Another Perspective

Neil Freeman

For another perspective on this famous speech, here is Neil Freeman's Folio version of the text with his commentary:

Speake the Speech I pray you, as I pronounc'd   3.2.1–45

Background: Just before the playing of the requested "The Murther of Gonzago" (with "some dosen or sixteene lines" added by Hamlet for Claudius's benefit), Hamlet seems to feel the need to instruct the actors in their business (or as the scholars suggest, Shakespeare felt the need to remind *his* own actors of *their* craft, which some of them seem to have neglected).

Style: general address to a small group
Where: somewhere near the great hall of the castle
To Whom: the first player and colleagues (an unspecified number)
# of Lines: 40   **Probable Timing:** 2.00 minutes

Hamlet 1   Speake the Speech I pray you, as I pronounc'd
it to you trippingly on the Tongue : But if you mouth it,
as many of your Players do, I had as live the Town-Cryer
had spoke my Lines : Nor do not saw the Ayre too much [ ]
your hand thus, but use all gently ; for in the verie Torrent,
Tempest, and (as I may say) the Whirle-winde of [ ]
Passion, you must acquire and beget a Temperance that
may give it Smoothnesse .

2   O it offends mee to the Soule, to
[see] a robustious Pery-wig-pated Fellow teare a Passion to tatters, to verie ragges, to split the eares of the
Groundlings : who (for the most part) are capeable of
nothing, but inexplicable dumbe shewes, & noise : I [could]
have such a Fellow whipt for o're-doing Termagant : it
out-Herod's Herod .

3   Pray you avoid it .

---

4 Be not too tame neyther : but let your owne
Discretion be your Tutor .

5   Sute the Action to the Word,
the Word to the Action, with this speciall observance : That
you [ore-stop] not the modestie of Nature ; for any
thing so [over-done], is [frö] the purpose of Playing, whose
end both at the first and now, was and is, to hold as 'twer

the Mirrour up to Nature ;   to shew Vertue her owne
Feature, Scorne her owne Image, and the verie Age and
Bodie of the Time, his forme and pressure .

6   Now, this
over-done, or come tardie off, though it [make] the unskil-
full laugh, cannot but make the Judicious greeve ; The
censure of the which One, must in your allowance o're-
way a whole Theater of Others .

7   Oh, there bee Players that
I have seene Play, and heard others praise, and that highly
(not to speake it prophanely) that neyther having the accent
of Christians, nor the [gate] of Christian, Pagan, [or Norman],
have so strutted and bellowed, that I have thought some
of Natures Jouerney-men had made men, and not made
them well, they imitated Humanity so abhominably .

---

8   And let those that
play your Clownes, speake no more [then] is set downe for
them .

9   For there be of them, that will themselves laugh,
to set on some quantitie of barren Spectators to laugh
too, though in the meane time, some necessary Question
of the Play be [then] to be considered : that's Villanous, &
shewes a most pittifull Ambition in the Foole that uses it .

10 Go make you readie .

The speech is essentially composed of two parts, Hamlet's instructions to the actors and his seemingly irrelevant digressions into his own reflections upon and reactions to what he regards as "bad acting"—and although commentators offer several contemporary explanations as to why, to satisfy an audience, there still must be a theatrical reason to justify these distractions. F's orthography shows that whereas the instructions are mainly intellectual, the sidebars are either emotional or passionate—the need to release seeming to be very important, perhaps suggesting his distress with all the bad real-life acting going on around him (Claudius, Rosincrance, Guildensterne, and even Ophelia).

- The importance of the forthcoming event is underscored by there being virtually no unembellished lines throughout the forty-one lines of advice and reminiscence until the very last words, F #10's "Go make you readie."

- The short F #3, "Pray you avoid it," is the other interesting exception, for both it and the very few surround phrases seem to go beyond just advice to the players, but reveal Hamlet's need for outward signs of honorable behavior from all around him:

> . Nor do not saw the Ayre too much [ ] your hand thus, but
>   use all gently ;
> : I could have such a Fellow whipt for o're-doing Termagant :
>   it out-Herod's Herod .
> : that's Villanous, & shewes a most pittifull Ambition in the
>   Foole that uses it .

- The opening advice of "Speake the Speech" is strongly intellectual (F #1, 15/6), only to be broken by strong emotion as he becomes sidetracked into expressing at length what "offends mee to the Soule" (5/9, F #2's first four and a half lines), while the thought of whipping the "Fellow" who offends him becomes totally intellectual (4/0 in F #2's last two surround phrase line and a half)

- After the quiet imploring of the short F #3, as Hamlet returns to his series of instructions his passions return (F #4, 2/2), which he quickly reins in, reestablishing intellectual control (21/9, F #5–6) for the remainder of his instructions

- But once more, as he breaks off into describing bad actors whose performances have offended him, his intellect gives way, this time to passion (8/9, F #7)

- Commentators acknowledge that F #8–9 is a contemporary reference to the "Clownes" of his own company improvising too much, so it's hardly surprising that this moment is first emotional (1/3, F #8), then with the intellectual elaboration (3/1, F #9's first three and a half lines), quickly turning to passion in his final surround phrase denunciation (3/3, F #9's last line and half)

- And after all the verbiage and sidetracks, as the time grows near for the performance that Hamlet hopes will reveal all, at last Hamlet becomes quiet (the unembellished F #10)

BRIEF BACKGROUND TO THE FIRST FOLIO

Neil Freeman

The First Folio

The end of 1623 saw the publication of the justifiably famed First Folio (F1). The single volume, published in a run of approximately one thousand copies at the princely sum of one pound (a tremendous risk, considering that a single play would sell at no more than six pence, one-fortieth of F1's price, and that the annual salary of a schoolmaster was only ten pounds), contained thirty-six plays.

The manuscripts from which each F1 play would be printed came from a variety of sources. Some had already been printed. Some came from the playhouse complete with production details. Some had no theatrical input at all but were handsomely copied out and easy to read. Some were supposedly very messy, complete with first draft scribbles and crossings out. Yet, as Charlton Hinman, the revered dean of First Folio studies, describes F1 in the Introduction to the Norton Facsimile:

> It is of inestimable value for what it is, for what it contains. For here are preserved the masterworks of the man universally recognized as our greatest writer; and preserved, as Ben Jonson realized at the time of the original publication, not for an age but for all time.

What Does F1 Represent?

- texts prepared for actors who rehearsed three days for a new play and one day for one already in the repertoire
- written in a style (rhetoric incorporating debate) so different from ours (grammatical) that many modern alterations based on grammar (or poetry) have done remarkable harm to the rhetorical/debate quality of the original text and thus to interpretations of characters
- written for an acting company the core of which steadily grew older, and whose skills and interests changed markedly over twenty years as well as for an audience whose makeup and interests likewise changed as the company grew more experienced

The whole is based upon supposedly the best documents available at the time, collected by men closest to Shakespeare throughout his career, and brought to a single printing house whose errors are now widely understood—far more than those of some of the printing houses that produced the original quartos.

The Key Question

What text have you been working with—a good modern text or an "original" text, that is, a copy of one of the first printings of the play?

If it's a modern text, no matter how well edited, despite all the learned information offered, it's not surprising that you feel somewhat at a loss, for there is a huge difference between the original printings (the First Folio and the individual quartos) and any text prepared after 1700 right up to the most modern of editions. All the post-1700 texts have been tidied up for the modern reader to ingest silently, revamped according to the rules of correct grammar, syntax, and poetry. However, the "originals" were prepared for actors speaking aloud, playing characters often in a great deal of emotional and/or intellectual stress, and were set down on paper according to the very flexible rules of rhetoric and a seemingly very cavalier attitude toward the rules of grammar, and syntax, and spelling, and capitalization, and even poetry.

Unfortunately, because of the grammatical and syntactical standardization in place by the early 1700s, many of the quirks and oddities of the original also have been dismissed as "accidental"—usually as compositor error either in deciphering the original manuscript, falling prey to their own particular idiosyncrasies, or not having calculated correctly the amount of space needed to set the text. Modern texts dismiss the possibility that these very quirks and oddities may be by Shakespeare, hearing his characters in as much difficulty as poor Peter Quince is in *A Midsummer Night's Dream* (when he, as the Prologue, terrified and struck down by stage fright, makes a huge grammatical hash in introducing his play "Pyramus and Thisbe" before the aristocracy, whose acceptance or rejection can make or break him):

> If we offend, it is with our good will.
> That you should think, we come not to offend,
> But with good will.

>   To show our simple skill,
> That is the true beginning of our end .
> Consider then, we come but in despite.
> We do not come, as minding to content you ,
> Our true intent is.
>   All for your delight
> We are not here.
>   That you should here repent you,
> The Actors are at hand; and by their show,
> You shall know all, that you are like to know.
>
> *(A Midsummer Night's Dream)*

In many other cases in the complete works what was originally printed is equally "peculiar," but, unlike Peter Quince, these peculiarities are usually regularized by most modern texts.

Most of these "peculiarities" resulted from Shakespeare setting down for his actors the stresses, trials, and tribulations the characters are experiencing as they think and speak, and thus are theatrical gold dust for the actor, director, scholar, teacher, and general reader alike.

The First Essential Difference between the Two Texts: Thinking

A **modern** text can show:

- the story line
- your character's conflict with the world at large
- your character's conflict with certain individuals within that world

but because of the very way an "original" text was set, it can show you all this plus one key extra, the very thing that makes big speeches what they are:

- the conflict within the character

Why?

Any good playwright writes about characters in stressful situations who are often in a state of conflict, not only with the world around them and the people in that world, but also within themselves. And you probably know from personal experience that when these conflicts occur, people do not necessarily utter the most perfect of grammatical/poetic/syntactic statements, phrases, or sentences. Joy and delight, pain and sorrow often come sweeping through in the way things are said, in the incoherence of the phrases, the running together of normally disassociated ideas, and even in the sounds of the words themselves.

The tremendous advantage of the period in which Shakespeare was setting his plays down on paper and how they first appeared in print was that when characters were rational and in control of self and situation, their phrasing and sentences (and poetic structure) would appear to be quite normal even to a modern eye—but when things were going wrong, these sentences and phrasing (and poetic structure) would become highly erratic. But the Quince-type eccentricities are rarely allowed to stand. Sadly, in tidying, most modern texts usually make the text far too clean, thus setting rationality when none originally existed.

The Second Essential Difference between First Folio and Modern Texts: Speaking, Arguing, Debating

Having discovered what and how you or your character is thinking is only the first stage of the work. You/the character then have to speak aloud, in a society that absolutely loved to speak—and not only speak ideas (content) but to speak entertainingly so as to keep listeners enthralled (and this was especially so when you have little content to offer and have to mask it somehow; think of today's television adverts and political spin doctors as a parallel, and you get the picture). Indeed one of the Elizabethan "how to win an argument" books was very precise about this: George Puttenham, *The Art of English Poesie* (1589).

Elizabethan Schooling

All educated classes could debate/argue at the drop of a hat, for both boys (in "petty-schools") and girls (by books and tutors) were trained in what was known overall as the art of rhetoric, which itself was split into three parts:

- First, how to distinguish the real from false appearances/outward show (think of the three caskets in *The Merchant of Venice* in which the lan-

guage on the gold and silver caskets enticingly, and deceptively, seems to offer hopes of great personal rewards that are dashed when the language is carefully explored, whereas once the apparent threat on the lead casket is carefully analyzed, the reward therein is the greatest that could be hoped for).
- Second, how to frame your argument on one of "three great grounds": honor/morality; justice/legality; and, when all else fails, expedience/practicality.
- Third, how to order and phrase your argument so winsomely that your audience will vote for you no matter how good the opposition—and there were well over two hundred rules and variations by which winning could be achieved, all of which had to be assimilated before a child's education was considered over and done with.

Thinking on Your Feet: That Is, The Quick, Deft, Rapid Modification of Each Tiny Thought

The Elizabethan—therefore, your character, and therefore, you—was also trained to explore and modify thoughts as they spoke—never would you see a sentence in its entirety and have it perfectly worked out in your mind before you spoke (unless it was a deliberately written, formal public declaration, as with the Officer of the Court in *The Winter's Tale*, reading the charges against Hermione). Thus, after uttering your very first phrase, you might expand it, or modify it, deny it, change it, and so on throughout the whole sentence and speech.

From the poet Samuel Taylor Coleridge, there is a wonderful description of how Shakespeare put thoughts together like "a serpent twisting and untwisting in its own strength," that is, with one thought springing out of the one previous. Treat each new phrase as a fresh unraveling of the serpent's coil. What is discovered (and therefore said) is only revealed as the old coil/phrase disappears, revealing a new coil in its place. The new coil is the new thought. The old coil moves/disappears because the previous phrase is finished with as soon as it is spoken.

Modern Application

It is very rarely that we speak dispassionately in our "real" lives. After all, thoughts give rise to feelings, feelings give rise to thoughts, and we usually speak both together—unless

1. we're trying very hard for some reason to control ourselves and not give ourselves away;

2. or the volcano of emotions within us is so strong that we cannot control ourselves, and feelings swamp thoughts;

3. and sometimes whether deliberately or unconsciously, we color words according to our feelings; the humanity behind the words so revealed is instantly understandable.

How the Original Texts Naturally Enhance/Underscore This Control or Release

The amazing thing about the way all Elizabethan/early Jacobean texts were first set down (the term used to describe the printed words on the page being "orthography"), is that it was flexible, allowing for such variations to be automatically set down without fear of grammatical repercussion.

So if Shakespeare heard Juliet's Nurse working hard to try to convince Juliet that the Prince's nephew Juliet is being forced to (bigamously) marry, instead of setting the everyday normal

> O he's a lovely gentleman

which the modern texts HAVE to set, the first printings were permitted to set

> O hee's a Lovely Gentleman

suggesting that something might be going on inside the Nurse that causes her to release such excessive energy.

Be Careful

This needs to be stressed very carefully: the orthography doesn't dictate to you/force you to accept exactly what it means. The orthography simply suggests that you might want to explore this moment further or more deeply.

In other words, simply because of the flexibility with which the Elizabethans/Shakespeare could set down on paper what they heard in their minds or wanted their listeners to hear, in addition to all the modern acting necessities of character—situation, objective, intention, action, and tactics—the original Shakespeare texts offer pointers to where feelings (either emotional or intellectual, or when combined together as passion, both) are also evident.

Summary

BASIC APPROACH TO FIRST FOLIO SPEECHES ON THE FOLLOWING PAGES:

1. First, use the modern version shown first. By doing so you can discover:

- the basic plot line of what's happening to the character
- the first set of conflicts/obstacles impinging on the character as a result of the situation or actions of other characters
- the supposed grammatical and poetical correctness of the speech

2. Then you can explore:

- any acting techniques you'd apply to any modern soliloquy, including establishing for the character
- the given circumstances of the scene
- their outward state of being (who they are sociologically, etc.)
- their intentions and objectives
- the resultant action and tactics they decide to pursue

3. When this is complete, consult the First Folio version of the text. This will help you discover and explore:

- the precise thinking and debating process so essential to an understanding of any Shakespeare text
- the moments when the text is *not* grammatically or poetically as correct as the modern texts would have you believe, which will in turn help you recognize the moments of conflict and struggle stemming from within the character itself
- the sense of fun and enjoyment Shakespeare's language nearly always offers you no matter how dire the situation

Should you wish to further explore even more the differences between the two texts, the commentary that follows discusses how the First Folio has been changed and what those alterations might mean for the human arc of the speech.

Notes on How the First Folio Speeches Are Set Up

Each of the scenes that follow consists of the modern text with commentary, as well as select speeches from the First Folio, which will include the background on the speech and other information including number of lines, approximate timing, and who is addressed.

PROBABLE TIMING: Shown on the page before the speech begins. 0.45 = a forty-five-second speech

Symbols & Abbreviations in the Commentary and Text

F: the First Folio

mt.: modern texts

F # followed by a number: the number of the sentence under discussion in the First Folio version of the speech; thus F #7 would refer to the seventh sentence

mt. # followed by a number: the number of the sentence under discussion in the modern text version of the speech, thus mt. #5 would refer to the fifth sentence

 # /# (e.g., 3/7): the first number refers to the number of capital letters in the passage under discussion; the second refers to the number of long spellings therein

/ within a quotation from the speech, the "/" symbol indicates where one verse line ends and a fresh one starts

[ ] : set around words in both texts when F1 sets one word, mt another

{ } : some minor alteration has been made, in a speech built up, where a word or phrase will be changed, added, or removed

{†} : this symbol shows where a sizable part of the text is omitted

Terms Found in the Commentary

OVERALL

1. **orthography**: the capitalization, spellings, punctuation of the First Folio

SIGNS OF IMPORTANT DISCOVERIES/ARGUMENTS WITHIN A FIRST FOLIO SPEECH

2. **major punctuation**: colons and semicolons: since the Shakespeare texts are based so much on the art of debate and argument, the importance of F1's major punctuation must not be underestimated, for both the semicolon (;) and colon (:) mark a moment of importance for the character, either for itself, as a moment of discovery or revelation, or as a key point in a discussion, argument, or debate that it wishes to impress upon other characters onstage.

As a rule of thumb:

a. the more frequent colon (:) suggests that whatever the power of the point discovered or argued, the character is not sidetracked and can continue with the argument—as such, the colon can be regarded as a **logical** connection

b. the far less frequent semicolon (;) suggests that because of the power inherent in the point discovered or argued, the character is sidetracked and momentarily loses the argument and falls back into itself or can only continue the argument with great difficulty—as such, the semicolon should be regarded as an **emotional** connection

3. **surround phrases**: phrase(s) surrounded by major punctuation, or a combination of major punctuation and the end or beginning of a sentence: thus these phrases seem to be of special importance for both character and speech, well worth exploring as key to the argument made and/or emotions released

A LOOSE RULE OF THUMB TO THE THINKING PROCESS OF A FIRST FOLIO CHARACTER

1. mental discipline/**intellect**: a section where capitals dominate suggests that the intellectual reasoning behind what is being spoken or discovered is of more concern than the personal response beneath it

2. feelings/**emotions**: a section where long spellings dominate suggests that the personal response to what is being spoken or discovered is of more concern than the intellectual reasoning behind it

3. **passion**: a section where both long spellings and capitals are present in almost equal proportions suggests that mind and emotion/feelings are inseparable, and thus the character is speaking passionately

SIGNS OF LESS THAN GRAMMATICAL THINKING WITHIN A FIRST FOLIO SPEECH

1. **onrush**: sometimes thoughts are coming so fast that several topics are joined together as one long sentence, suggesting that the F character's mind is working very quickly, or that his/her emotional state is causing some concern. Most modern texts split such a sentence into several grammatically correct parts (the opening speech of *As You Like It* is a fine example, where F's long eighteen-line opening sentence is split into six), while the modern texts' resetting may be syntactically correct, the F moment is nowhere near as calm as the revisions suggest.

2. **fastlink**: sometimes F shows thoughts moving so quickly for a character that the connecting punctuation between disparate topics is merely a comma, suggesting that there is virtually no pause in springing from one idea to the next. Unfortunately, most modern texts rarely allow this to stand, instead replacing the obviously disturbed comma with a grammatical period, once more creating calm that it seems the original texts never intended to show.

FIRST FOLIO SIGNS OF WHEN VERBAL GAME PLAYING HAS TO STOP

1. **nonembellished**: a section with neither capitals nor long spellings suggests that what is being discovered or spoken is so important to the character that there is no time to guss it up with vocal or mental excesses: an unusual moment of self-control.

2. **short sentence**: coming out of a society where debate was second nature, many of Shakespeare's characters speak in long sentences in which ideas are stated, explored, redefined, and summarized, all before moving on to the next idea in the argument, discovery, or debate. The longer sentence is the sign of a rhetorically trained mind used to public speaking (oratory), but at times an idea or discovery is so startling or inevitable that length is either unnecessary or impossible to maintain: hence the occasional very important short sentence suggests that there is no time for the niceties of oratorical adornment with which to sugar the pill—verbal games are at an end, and now the basic core of the issue must be faced.

3. **monosyllabic**: with English being composed of two strands, the polysyllabic (stemming from French, Italian, Latin, and Greek), and

the monosyllabic (from the Anglo-Saxon), each strand has two distinct functions: the polysyllabic words are often used when there is time for fanciful elaboration and rich description (which could be described as "excessive rhetoric") while the monosyllabic occur when, literally, there is no other way of putting a basic question or comment: Juliet's "Do you love me? I know thou wilt say aye" is a classic example of both monosyllables and non-embellishment. With monosyllables, only the naked truth is being spoken; nothing is hidden.

SCENE STUDY

Act IV, Scene iii

Cassius and Brutus

☙❧

Marcus Brutus and Caius Cassius, two principal conspirators in the assassination of Julius Caesar, the Roman Emperor, now meet in Brutus's tent in preparation for their battle against Octavius Caesar and Mark Antony. A guard is set at the entrance to ensure their privacy.

CASSIUS

> That you have wronged me doth appear in this:
> You have condemned and noted Lucius Pella
> For taking bribes here of the Sardians,
> Wherein my letters, praying on his side
> Because I knew the man, was slighted off.   5

BRUTUS

> You wronged yourself to write in such a case.

CASSIUS

> In such a time as this it is not meet
> That every nice offense should bear his comment.

BRUTUS

> Let me tell you Cassius, you yourself
> Are much condemned to have an itching palm   10

---

2 **noted** publicly disgraced
4 **praying...side** appealing on his behalf
5 **slighted off** slightly dismissed
8 **nice** unimportant; **his** its **comment** scrutiny
10 **condemned to have** accused of having

Act IV, Scene iii (Cassius and Brutus)

    To sell and mart your offices for gold
    To undeservers.

CASSIUS   I an itching palm?
    You know that you are Brutus that speaks this
    Or by the gods this speech were else your last.

BRUTUS
    The name of Cassius honors this corruption   15
    And chastisement doth therefore hide his head.

CASSIUS
    Chastisement!

BRUTUS
    Remember March, the ides of March remember.
    Did not great Julius bleed for justice' sake?
    What villain touched his body that did stab   20
    And not for justice? What, shall one of us
    That struck the foremost man of all this world
    But for supporting robbers, shall we now
    Contaminate our fingers with base bribes
    And sell the mighty space of our large honors   25
    For so much trash as may be grasped thus?
    I had rather be a dog and bay the moon
    Than such a Roman.

CASSIUS   Brutus bait not me;
    I'll not endure it. You forget yourself

---

11 **mart** deal in; **offices** official position
12 **itching palm** covetous nature
15 **honors** lends respectability to
18 **ides of March** March 15th (the day Caesar was assassinated)
21 **And not** except
23 **supporting robbers** protecting corrupt officials
25 **mighty … honors** great potential of our patronage
26 **trash** rubbish/money (contemptuous)
27 **bay** howl against
28 **bait** harass (bears were baited at the stake)

>   To hedge me in. I am a soldier, I,   30
> Older in practice, abler than yourself
> To make conditions.

BRUTUS   Go to! You are not, Cassius.

CASSIUS

> I am.

BRUTUS

> I say you are not.

CASSIUS

> Urge me no more, I shall forget myself;   35
> Have mind upon your health, tempt me no farther.

BRUTUS Away, slight man!

CASSIUS Is't possible?

BRUTUS   Hear me, for I will speak.
> Must I give way and room to your rash choler?
> Shall I be frighted when a madman stares?   40

CASSIUS

> O ye gods, ye gods! Must I endure all this?

BRUTUS

> All this? Ay more: fret till your proud heart break.
> Go show your slaves how choleric you are
> And make your bondmen tremble. Must I budge?
> Must I observe you? Must I stand and crouch   45

---

30 **hedge me in** confine, limit me
32 **make conditions** manage business
35 **Urge** incite, press
36 **tempt** try, test
37 **slight** insignificant
39 **way and room** free course and scope; **rash choler** quick temper
40 **stares** glares
44 **budge** flinch
45 **observe** humor, pay respect to; **crouch** i.e., bow

Act IV, Scene iii (Cassius and Brutus)

Under your testy humor? By the gods
You shall digest the venom of your spleen
Though it do split you, for from this day forth
I'll use you for my mirth, yea for my laughter,
When you are waspish.

CASSIUS Is it come to this? 50

BRUTUS
You say you are a better soldier:
Let it appear so, make your vaunting true
And it shall please me well. For mine own part,
I shall be glad to learn of noble men.

CASSIUS
You wrong me every way, you wrong me Brutus: 55
I said an elder soldier, not a better.
Did I say, better?

BRUTUS If you did, I care not.

CASSIUS
When Caesar lived, he durst not thus have moved me.

BRUTUS
Peace, peace, you durst not so have tempted him.

CASSIUS
I durst not? 60

BRUTUS
No.

---

46 **testy humor** irritability
47 **digest...spleen** swallow the poison from your bad temper
49 **for my mirth...laughter** as an object of fun and ridicule
52 **vaunting** boasting
54 **learn of** be instructed by
58 **moved** angered
59 **tempted** provoked

CASSIUS
What? Durst not tempt him?

BRUTUS For your life you durst not.

CASSIUS
Do not presume too much upon my love;
I may do that I shall be sorry for.

BRUTUS
You have done that you should be sorry for. 65
There is no terror, Cassius, in your threats;
For I am armed so strong in honesty
That they pass by me as the idle wind
Which I respect not. I did send to you
For certain sums of gold which you denied me; 70
For I can raise no money by vile means.
By heaven, I had rather coin my heart
And drop my blood for drachmas than to wring
From the hard hands of peasants their vile trash
By any indirection. I did send 75
To you for gold to pay my legions
Which you denied me. Was that done like Cassius?
Should I have answered Caius Cassius so?
When Marcus Brutus grows so covetous
To lock such rascal counters from his friends, 80
Be ready gods with all your thunderbolts—
Dash him to pieces!

CASSIUS I denied you not.

---

67 **honesty** integrity
69 **respect not** ignore
73 **drachmas** i.e., money
75 **indirection** devious means
80 **rascal counters** worthless coins

Act IV, Scene iii (Cassius and Brutus)

BRUTUS
You did.

CASSIUS   I did not. He was but a fool
That brought my answer back. Brutus hath rived my heart.
A friend should bear his friend's infirmities   85
But Brutus makes mine greater than they are.

BRUTUS
I do not till you practice them on me.

CASSIUS
You love me not.

BRUTUS   I do not like your faults.

CASSIUS
A friendly eye could never see such faults.

BRUTUS
A flatterer's would not though they do appear   90
As huge as high Olympus.

CASSIUS
Come Antony and young Octavius come,
Revenge yourselves alone on Cassius,
For Cassius is aweary of the world:
Hated by the one he loves, braved by his brother,   95
Checked like a bondman, all his faults observed,
Set in a notebook, learned and conned by rote
To cast into my teeth. O I could weep
My spirit from mine eyes! There is my dagger
And here my naked breast, within a heart   100

---

84 **rived** split
91 **Olympus** (legendary home of the Greek gods)
93 **alone** only
95 **braved** challenged, opposed
96 **Checked** rebuked
97 **conned by rote** learned by heart
98 **cast . . . teeth** throw in my face

Dearer than Pluto's mine, richer than gold:
If that thou be'st a Roman, take it forth.
I that denied thee gold, will give my heart.
Strike as thou didst at Caesar for I know
When thou didst hate him worst, thou lovedst him better   105
Than thou ever lovedst Cassius.

BRUTUS   Sheathe your dagger.
Be angry when you will, it shall have scope.
Do what you will, dishonor shall be humor.
O Cassius you are yoked with a lamb
That carries anger as a flint bears fire   110
Who, much enforced, shows a hasty spark
And straight is cold again.

CASSIUS   Hath Cassius lived
To be but mirth and laughter to his Brutus
When grief and blood ill-tempered vexeth him?

BRUTUS
When I spoke that I was ill-tempered too.   115

CASSIUS
Do you confess so much? Give me your hand.

BRUTUS
And my heart too.

CASSIUS   O Brutus!

BRUTUS   What's the matter?

---

101 **Dearer** more precious; **Pluto** (god of the underworld; often confused with Plutus, god of riches)
107 **scope** free play
108 **dishonor ... humor** insults will be as if a whim, idiosyncrasy
111 **Who** which; **much enforced** strongly provoked / struck
112 **straight** immediately
114 **ill-tempered** ill-balanced

Act IV, Scene iii (Cassius and Brutus)

CASSIUS
Have not you love enough to bear with me
When that rash humor which my mother gave me
Makes me forgetful?

BRUTUS   Yes Cassius, and from henceforth   120
When you are over-earnest with your Brutus,
He'll think your mother chides and leave you so.

> 119 **rash humor** hasty temperament
> 122 **leave you so** let it go at that

Rehearsing the Scene

This quarrel springs immediately to life. Both characters know they can be overheard by sentries outside the tent, and this knowledge prevents a loud climax from coming too soon.

The characters are clearly and boldly contrasted, each providing a self-portrait that can be used by actors as a point of departure for exploration. Brutus says he is "a lamb / That carries anger as the flint bears fire / Who, much enforced, shows a hasty spark / And straight is cold again." (ll. 109–122)

Brutus's emotion in this scene must burst through a customary self-promotion and discipline in argument and debate. He tries to be self-aware at all times: "Let me tell you . . . Hear me, for I will speak . . . For I am armed so strong in honesty . . . When Marcus Brutus grows so covetous . . . " (ll. 9, 8, 67, and 79).

Cassius says about himself, ". . . that rash humor which my mother gave me / Makes me forgetful." (ll. 119–20) He is naturally quick and passionate; his most sustained argument is laced with exclamations and shows of temperament.

The energy in their conflict will be enhanced by the actors' response to textual variations of tone, pitch, syntax, vocabulary, and meter. When the two characters use the same words, picking up ideas from each other, they turn them to their own advantage, changing the implications and rhythms (for Brutus, see lines 6, 42, 51, 59, and 65; for Cassius, lines 12, 17, 56, 60, and 82). Metrical changes define thrusts and parries. When thoughts are most violently opposed, they share a single verse line, so that the second speaker responds to the first by taking over and changing the rhythms already established: see lines 12, 28, 32, 38, 50, 57, 62, 82, 83, 88. On three crucial occasions, a half-line is left uncompleted, so marking a silence and change of mood; so the duelists disengage, following a particularly violent thrust. On two occasions the metrical basis for speech seems to break down entirely, at lines 33–34 and 60–61: perhaps these metrical crises could be taken very quickly, recklessly and instinctively. Or a long silence might be held between the two speeches; or one speaker or both might speak very slowly, weighing each word carefully.

Line 84 is a special metrical problem because it has twelve syllables. Either the actor must pack the long line into the tensyllable norm, or he should treat the line as two incomplete verse lines so that Cassius takes a pause in the middle of his reply to Brutus. This could be an instance of his "rashness", or a moment when he masters his instinct for a hasty reply.

Immediately after this exceptional metrical crux, Cassius forces an entirely new level of consciousness to the scene by talking of his "heart" and of "friends", and by proceeding to the simple challenge "You love me not" (1. 87). (His earlier mention of "love" at line 63 had been summarily swept aside.) Brutus attempts to deflect Cassius's emotional tone, but Cassius will have none of it as he offers his dagger and sets the emotional stakes even higher. In grappling with Cassius's histrionic action, the actor must well understand the character's motive. Is this a bit of melodramatic bravado? Clearly here Cassius is attempting to regain control of the scene, but resorting to such a drastic action may evidence a lack of control. Does Cassius know that it is nearly absurd, in its suddenness and melodramatic impracticality, and does he calculate that this is likely to impress the self-important Brutus? Or is Cassius so "rash" and "over-earnest" that he truly means what he does, and intends it to be taken literally? When he says, with Brutus-like self-awareness, that "Cassius is aweary of the world" (l. 94), is he honestly asking Brutus to kill him? Is he close to tears as lines 98–99 suggest? To act this moment truthfully, the actor will have to sense Cassius' deepest instincts; simple notions of his "rashness" will not be sufficient.

Why does Brutus change at this point? Does Cassius expose himself here in a way that his "friend" finds irresistible? Does Brutus *need* friendship, love and trust, despite his talk about justice, honor and his ability as a soldier? Is he able to dismiss Cassius to dishonor among "slaves" and "bondmen" (11. 43–44), but unable to face him on his own without reconciliation of their differences? Do Cassius's emotional appeals bring out a different side of Brutus?

This quarrel scene is justly famous: it has both fire and mystery.

First Folio Speeches

For another perspective, following are speeches in this scene from the First Folio with commentary by Neil Freeman drawn from the *Once More Unto the Speech* series.

BRUTUS YOU WRONG'D YOUR SELFE TO WRITE IN SUCH A CASE.

Background: In his funeral oration Antony has succeeded in turning the crowd against the conspirators who have fled from Rome. Octavius, Caesar's nephew, has been welcomed into Rome, and a tripartite leadership agreement to restore order and defeat the conspirators has been arranged between himself and the insignificant Lepidus. In the meantime the conspirators are attempting to levy support, money, and men to withstand the inevitable tripartite-led war against them. In so doing Cassius is prepared to support his men who cut corners to get what they want, including one Lucius Pella accused of bribery, even writing letters of support on their behalf, which leads "honourable" Brutus to speak as follows.

Style: As part of a two-handed scene.

Where: Brutus's battlefield tent.

To Whom: Cassius.

# of Lines: 18 **Probable Timing:** 0.55 minutes

Brutus

1 You wrong'd your selfe to write in such a case.

_____

2 Let me tell you Cassius, you your selfe
   Are much condemn'd to have an itching Palme,
   To sell, and Mart your Offices for Gold
   To Undeservers.

_____

3   The name of Cassius Honors this corruption,
    And Chasticement doth therefore hide his head .

---

4   Remember March, the Ides of March remember :
    Did not great Julius bleede for Justice sake?

5   What Villaine touch'd his body, that did stab,
    And not for Justice?

6   What?

7   Shall one of Us,
    That strucke the Formost man of all this World,
    But for supporting Robbers : shall we now,
    Contaminate our fingers, with base Bribes?
    And sell the mighty space of our large Honors
    For so much trash, as may be grasped thus?

8   I had rather be a Dogge, and bay the Moone,
    [Then] such a Roman .

F's orthography shows how well Brutus is able to control his emotions and stay highly factually / intellectual focused in his "Chasticement" of Cassius, almost until the end of the speech.

• The fact that there are no surround phrases and just one piece of major punctuation suggests that this speech (highly intellectual until the last sentence) comes springing forth without premeditation, making its lack of emotional release even more remarkable.

• With such a springing-forth, the lack of released emotion (22/6 the first sixteen lines of the speech) provides great witness to how much Brutus wishes to let the facts speak for themselves rather than let his heart do the work for him.

• However, the sudden passion of the final sentence (F #8, 3/2) suggests just how much of a strain this causes him, especially since the outburst has been preceded by three extra breath-thoughts that appear in the middle of F #7 as the appalling thought of "shall we now / Contaminate our fingers, with base Bribes". The extra breaths suggest that Brutus is either taking great care to get the final points across and / or is almost speechless at the points he must now utter.

Act IV, Scene iii (Cassius and Brutus) 53

- That the speech opens with a short, one-line, monosyllabic sentence shows with what a tight rein Brutus is holding himself in check.
- The few occasions of emotion that do break through deal in concepts of honor and its besmirching, with the moment of Caesar's death—"Did not great Julius bleede for Justice sake"—being matched against the rumors of Cassius accepting bribes ("your selfe / Are much condemn'd to have an itching Palme") and against any "Villaine" that touched Caesar's body for anything other than "Justice".

CASSIUS   A FRIEND SHOULD BEARE HIS FRIENDS INFIRMITIES ;

Background: Despite Brutus's attack, Cassius goes off on an emotional tangent, preceding the following with "Brutus hath riv'd my hart".

Style: As part of a two-handed scene.

Where: Brutus's battlefield tent.

To Whom: Brutus.

# of Lines: 17   **Probable Timing:** 0.55 minutes

Cassius

1   A Friend should beare his Friends infirmities ;
    But Brutus makes mine greater [then] they are .

---

2   Come Antony, and yong Octavius come,
    Revenge your selves alone on Cassius,
    For Cassius is a-weary of the World :
    Hated by one he loves, brav'd by his Brother,
    Check'd like a bondman, all his faults observ'd,
    Set in a Note-booke, learn'd, and con'd by roate
    To cast into my Teeth .

3   O I could weepe
    My Spirit from mine eyes .

4   There is a Dagger,
    And heere my naked Breast : Within, a Heart
    Deerer [then] Pluto's Mine, Richer [then] Gold :
    If that thou bee'st a Roman, take it foorth .

5   I that deny'd thee Gold, will give my Heart :
      Strike as thou did'st at Caesar : for I know,
      When thou did'st hate him worst, [ÿ] loved'st him better
      [Then] ever thou loved'st Cassius .

Given Cassius' reputation as a hothead, this is a remarkable attempt to keep himself under control, perhaps an attempt to match Brutus's rebuke that forces this response (Brutus's speech above). However, the surround phrases opening and closing the speech and the sudden non-intellectual outbursts clearly show both how much Cassius has to do to keep himself under control and where he fails to do so.

- Not surprisingly, despite F #1's intellectual orthography (3/1), the two surround phrases opening the speech have an emotional underpinning, linked as they are by the only semicolon in the speech: " . A Friend should beare his Friends infirmities ; / But Brutus makes mine greater then they are . "

- The melodramatic imagery of F #2's opening three-line invitation for their enemies to take revenge on Cassius alone is offset by being completely intellectual (5/0)—perhaps this is a genuine realization, not an emotional bleat.

- The explanation why (supposedly being hated by Brutus) undoes this by spinning into passion (3/2, ending F #2), which leads to the one short passionate sentence (F #3, 1/1) "O I could weepe / My Spirit from mine eyes . " Both show the emotional battle Cassius is struggling to contain.

- Which leads to intellectual determination (13/5 F #4–5) highlighted by the five consecutive surround phrases forming F #4 and the line and a half opening F #5: " . There is a Dagger, / And heere my naked Breast : Within, a Heart / Deerer then Pluto's Mine, Richer then Gold : / If that thou bee'st a Roman, take it foorth . / I that deny'd thee Gold, will give my Heart : / Strike as thou did'st at Caesar : "

- This determination again removes the potential for melodrama, but not completely, for the end of each of the last two sentences betrays his control, with the one line outburst ending F #4—"If thou bee'st a Roman, take it [i.e., Cassius's dagger] foorth'—slipping into passion and the two-and-a-half-line notion ending F #5, of Brutus loving Caesar more than he ever did Cassius, becoming emotional (2/4 all told).

Working on Modern and First Folio Texts

Paul Sugarman

It is important when working on text that you gain information from modern edited texts, such as the Applause Shakespeare Library, which can provide much information on understanding what is happening in the scene, and then look at the original printed texts of the First Folio, such as the Applause First Folio Editions, which can give additional insights.

So on the pages that follow, we look at several of the key moments in the play: Cassius and Brutus's first conversation in Act I, Portia and Brutus's confrontation after the departure of the conspirators, and Antony's funeral speech. We first look at them as they appear in the Applause Shakespeare Library and then as rendered in *Once More Unto the Speech* by Neil Freeman.

Act I, Scene ii: Modern Text

Flourish, and shout

BRUTUS What means this shouting?
I do fear, the people Choose Caesar 80
For their king.

CASSIUS   Ay, do you fear it?
Then must I think you would not have it so.

BRUTUS I would not, Cassius; yet I love him well.
But wherefore do you hold me here so long?
What is it that you would impart to me?   85
If it be aught toward the general good,°
Set honor in one eye and death i' the other,
And I will look on both indifferently,°
For let the gods so speed me° as I love
The name of honor more than I fear death.   90

CASSIUS I know that virtue to be in you, Brutus,
As well as I do know your outward favor.°
Well, honor is the subject of my story.
I cannot tell what you and other men
Think of this life; but, for my single self,   95
I had as lief not be° as live to be
In awe of such a thing as I myself.°
I was born free as Caesar; so were you:
We both have fed as well, and we can both
Endure the winter's cold as well as he: 100
For once, upon a raw and gusty day,
The troubled Tiber chafing with° her shores,
Caesar said to me "Dar'st thou, Cassius, now
Leap in with me into this angry flood,
And swim to yonder point?" Upon the word,   105
Accoutred as I was, I plungèd in
And bade him follow; so indeed he did.
The torrent roared, and we did buffet it
With lusty sinews, throwing it aside
And stemming° it with hearts of controversy;   110
But ere we could arrive° the point proposed,
Caesar cried "Help me, Cassius, or I sink!"
I, as Aeneas,° our great ancestor,
Did from the flames of Troy upon his shoulder

Act I, Scene ii (Brutus, Cassius) 57

79–90 They are interrupted by trumpets and shouting from the direction of the racecourse, and Brutus inadvertently reveals that he fears Caesar will be chosen king. Cassius pounces on this, and with "Then must I think would not have it so," he directly confronts Brutus with a searching question. Brutus admits his fears, but then he takes the bull by the horns and bluntly demands what Cassius wants of him, charging that it be "for the general good," and consistent with the "name of honor."

public welfare

impartially
make prosper

91–132 Cassius begins his denigration of Caesar with a stout assertion that, for himself, he cannot bear to be forced to look up to someone no better than he is. He then tells a story that shows Caesar as a braggart who has to be pulled out of the Tiber as a result of the consequences of his own folly, followed by a slighting reference to Caesar's fever in Spain. The pettiness of these attacks demonstrates the degree of Cassius's envy and of his hurt pride.

appearance, especially of the face

would just as soon not be alive
i.e., a mere mortal like myself

133–178 Another shout and flourish of trumpets interrupts him, confirming Brutus's fear that the public is giving Caesar some new honor. Cassius proceeds to compare Brutus and Caesar as equally worthy, and passionately denounces the present age for putting up with the domination of a mere man who takes upon himself the prerogatives of kingship. Brutus quietly hears him out. When Cassius finally comes to a fiery conclusion, Brutus thanks him for his regard, assures him he will consider what has been said and will, in time, give his answer. He cannot help, it would seem, adding that he too is not about to put up with what seems to lie ahead. Throughout this scene between Cassius and Brutus—two men earnestly talking, in contrast to the bustle and ceremony which has gone before—there is a contrast between the impassioned, vivid speech of the mercurial Cassius and the steady, reasoned utterance of Brutus. This makes the touches of feeling which break through Brutus's calm—his

raging against

making headway against
arrive at

legendary founder of Rome (hero of Virgil's *Aeneid*)

The old Anchises° bear, so from the waves of Tiber 115
Did I the tired Caesar. And this man
Is now become a god, and Cassius is
A wretched creature and must bend his body,
If Caesar carelessly but nod on him.
He had a fever when he was in Spain, 120
And when the fit° was on him, I did mark
How he did shake. 'Tis true, this god did shake;
His coward lips did from their color° fly,
And that same eye whose bend° doth awe the world
Did lose his° lustre. I did hear him groan: 125
Ay, and that tongue of his that bade the Romans
Mark him and write his speeches in their books,
Alas, it cried "Give me some drink, Tintinius,"
As a sick girl. Ye gods, it doth amaze° me
A man of such a feeble temper° should 130
So get the start of° the majestic world
And bear the palm° alone. *[Shout. Flourish]*

BRUTUS Another general shout!
I do believe that these applauses are
For some new honours that are heap'd on Caesar. 135

CASSIUS Why, man, he doth bestride the narrow world
Like a Colossus,° and we petty men
Walk under his huge legs and peep about
To find ourselves dishonourable graves.
Men at some time are masters of their fates. 140
The fault, dear Brutus, is not in our stars,
But in ourselves, that we are underlings.
"Brutus" and "Caesar." What should be in that "Caesar"?
Why should that name be sounded° more than yours?
Write them together, yours is as fair a name; 145
Sound them, it doth become the mouth as well.
Weigh them, it is as heavy. conjure with 'em,
"Brutus" will start° a spirit as soon as "Caesar."
Now, in the names of all the gods at once,
Upon what meat° doth this our Caesar feed 150
That he is grown so great? Age, thou art shamed.
Rome, thou hast lost the breed of noble bloods.°
When went there by an age, since the great flood,°
But it was famed with more than with one man?
When could they say till now, that talk'd of Rome, 155

Act I, Scene ii (Brutus, Cassius)   59

father of Aeneas   expressions of concern at the shouts and his "Brutus had rather be a villager" comment—all the more telling. Cassius, it seems, brings the conversation to a close, well satisfied with the result.

ague
natural color (i.e., red) /
   flag
glance
its

bewilder, stupefy
temperament
outstrip
Roman emblem of victory

bronze statue of Apollo,
   more than 100 feet
   high, that spanned the
   harbor of Rhodes

pronounced / resounded /
   proclaimed

rouse

a general Elizabethan
   word for food
persons of spirit
Zeus destroyed all of
   mankind by flood except
   Deucalion and Pyrrha

That her wide walls encompass'd but one man?
Now is it Rome indeed and room° enough,
When there is in it but one only man.
O, you and I have heard our fathers say,
There was a Brutus° once that would have brooked°   160
The eternal devil to keep his state° in Rome
As easily as a king.

BRUTUS That you do love me, I am nothing jealous;°
What you would work me to, I have some aim;°
How I have thought of this and of these times,   165
I shall recount hereafter; for this present,
I would not so° — with love I might entreat you—
Be any further moved.° What you have said
I will consider; what you have to say
I will with patience hear, and find a time   170
Both meet° to hear and answer such high things.
Till then, my noble friend, chew upon° this:
Brutus had rather be a villager
Than to repute himself a son of Rome
Under these hard conditions as° this time   175
Is like to lay upon us.

CASSIUS I am glad that my weak words
Have struck but thus much show of fire° from Brutus.

Act I, Scene ii (Brutus, Cassius)

(pun on *Rome* / *room*, which
 were pronounced alike)
Lucius Junius Brutus, who
 drove the Tarquins from
 Rome
endured
royal court

suspicious, doubtful
guess, conjecture

thus
urged

fitting
ruminate / ponder

which

(Brutus is imagined as the
 flint)

Act I, Scene ii: First Folio Speeches

Cassius   **I Know that vertue to be in you Brutus,**

Background: This is Brutus's response to Cassius's initial overtures; his very-much-to-the-point question "Into what dangers, would you / Lead me Cassius?", plus his comment that the first set of flourishes and shouts from the Capitol makes him "feare, the People choose Caesar / For their King", gives Cassius the needed opening to begin exploring the more serious, possibly even treasonous, matter at hand.

Style: As part of a two-handed scene.

Where: A street in Rome.

To Whom: Brutus.

# of Lines: 42   **Probable Timing:** 2.00 minutes

Cassius

1   I know that vertue to be in you Brutus,
    As well as I do know your outward favour .

2   Well, Honor is the subject of my Story :
    I cannot tell, what you and other men
    Thinke of this life : But for my single selfe,
    I had as liefe not be, as live to be
    In awe of such a Thing, as I my selfe .

3   I was borne free as Caesar, so were you,
    We both have fed as well, and we can both
    Endure the Winters cold, as well as hee .

4   For once, upon a Rawe and Gustie day,
    The troubled [Tyber], chafing with her Shores,
    Caesar saide to me, Dar'st thou Cassius now
    Leape in with me into this angry Flood,
    And swim to yonder Point?

5   Upon the word,
    Accoutred as I was, I plunged in,
    And bad him follow : so indeed he did .

Act I, Scene ii (Brutus, Cassius) 63

6   The Torrent roar'd, and we did buffet it
    With lusty Sinewes, throwing it aside,
    And stemming it with hearts of Controversie.

7   But ere we could arrive the Point propos'd,
    Caesar cride, Helpe me Cassius, or I sinke .

8   I (as Æneas, our great Ancestor,
    Did from the Flames of Troy, upon his shoulder
    The old [Anchyses] beare so, from the waves of [Tyber]
    Did I the tyred Caesar : And this Man,
    Is now become a God, and Cassius is
    A wretched Creature, and must bend his body,
    If Caesar carelesly but nod on him .

9   He had a Feaver when he was in Spaine,
    And when the Fit was on him, I did marke
    How he did shake : Tis true, this God did shake,
    His Coward lippes did from their colour flye,
    And that same Eye, whose bend doth awe the World,
    Did loose his Lustre : I did heare him grone :
    [I], and that Tongue of his, that bad the Romans
    Marke him, and write his Speeches in their Bookes,
    Alas, it cried, Give me some drinke Titinius,
    As a sicke Girle : Ye Gods, it doth amaze me,
    A man of such a feeble temper should
    So get the start of the Majesticke world,
    And beare the Palme alone .

Most modern texts undo two important clues by altering F's sentence pattern into a supposedly more rational structure. With F setting F #3 and #4 as separate sentences, the importance of each—F #3's statement that he (and presumably Brutus) should be regarded as Caesar's equal, and F #4's setting up the first story of Caesar's weakness—are highlighted as separate facts in and of themselves. Most modern texts jam the two sentences together as shown, reducing the power of each to a more general rant, which in fact comes later. But F's onrushed last sentence (#9) suggests that it is only now that Cassius seems to rant. Modern texts split F #9 in two, setting up a much more rational finish for Cassius than originally set.

- The speech starts quite firmly, with the intellect (3/1) of the first three lines culminating in F #2's opening surround phrase reassuring Brutus that " . Well, Honor is the subject of my Story : "

- But his attempt to control himself as the "Story" starts—"I cannot tell, what you and other men"—rapidly disappears, first into emotion (2/4 in F #2's remaining three lines) as he continues his self-definition, and then into passion as he begins to compare himself with Caesar (2/2 the three lines of F #3).

- Cassius's first steps towards proving his contention, F #4's challenge to swim the "troubled Tyber", are determinedly strongly intellectual (8/4), and then very quiet as he describes how he leapt in first. The totally unembellished F #5 ends via the surround phrase " : so indeed he did . ", possibly underscoring how fixed this incident is in his memory, or how carefully he is attempting to ensnare Brutus in his honor-serving tale.

- The first detailing of the actual swim (as "the Torrent roar'd") starts factually (F #6, 3/1), and extra breath-thoughts seen first in F #2 start to appear more frequently, as if Cassius is taking great care to underscore the smallest of points in order to enhance his case.

- Caesar's weakness (F #7 and the first three and a half lines of F #8) and Cassius's rescue of him are recalled passionately (10/7).

- However, the resultant denigration of Caesar having "now become a God" is totally intellectual (6/0 the last three and a half lines of F #8), presumably to ensure that personal feelings do not get in the way of Brutus's receiving the full force of Cassius's judgment.

- But the passions come sweeping back in as Cassius adds in a second example of Caesar's lack of backbone, the "Feaver when he was in Spaine": the first outlining of it (9/7 in just the first five and a half lines of F #9) is momentarily interrupted by an emotional monosyllabic surround phrase adding his own amazed description—" : I did heare him grone : "—and then the passions flow uninterrupted (11/8) through the last seven lines ending the speech as Cassius once more describes Caesar's behavior "as a sicke Girle" and then expresses his amazement that Caesar should hold "the Majesticke world" by himself "alone".

Act I, Scene ii (Brutus, Cassius)

CASSIUS   WHY MAN, HE DOTH BESTRIDE THE NARROW WORLD

Background: Brutus does not directly respond to Cassius's initial anti-Caesar diatribe, but instead seems disturbed by the fact that the further shouting from the Capitol could well signify "these applauses are / For some new honors, that are heap'd on Caesar". Cassius immediately takes advantage of this to press home his argument even further.

Style: As part of a two-handed scene.

Where: A street in Rome.

To Whom: Brutus.

# of Lines: 27   **Probable Timing:** 1.30 minutes

Cassius

1   Why man, he doth bestride the narrow world
     Like a Colossus, and we petty men
     Walke under his huge legges, and peepe about
     To finde our selves dishonourable Graves .

2   Men at sometime, are Masters of their Fates .

3   The fault (deere Brutus) is not in our Starres,
     But in our Selves, that we are underlings .

4   Brutus and Caesar: What should be in that Caesar?

5   Why should that name be sounded more [then] yours :
     Write them together : Yours, is as faire a Name :
     Sound them, it doth become the mouth aswell :
     Weigh them, it is as heavy : Conjure with 'em,
     Brutus will start a Spirit as soone as Caesar,
     Now in the names of all the Gods at once,
     Upon what meate doth this our Caesar feede,
     That he is growne so great?

6   Age, thou art sham'd .

7   Rome, thou hast lost the breed of Noble Bloods .

8   When went there by an Age, since the great Flood,
     But it was fam'd with more [then] with one man?

9 When could they say (till now) that talk'd of Rome,
   That her wide Walkes incompast but one man?
10 Now it is Rome indeed, and Roome enough
   When there is in it but one onely man .
11 O! you and I, have heard our Fathers say,
   There was a Brutus once, that would have brook'd
   Th'eternall Divell to keepe his State in Rome,
   As easily as a King .

In this, the immediate follow-up to his earlier speech above, Cassius seems to employ different tactics in his attempt to win Brutus. Now when he diminishes Caesar, he initially makes a great use of quiet unembellished lines to drive his points home (F #1–8), and then, from F #8 on, he uses at least seven extra breath-thoughts to ensure even the smallest of points are inescapably understood.

• The unembellished lines start with the very first Caesar-denigrating line: "Why man, he doth bestride the narrow world".

• Then come the personal Brutus-flattering surround-phrase implications from the top of F #4 through to F #5: "Brutus and Caesar : What should be in that Caesar ? / Why should that name be sounded more then yours : / Write them together : Yours, is as faire a Name : / Sound them, it doth become the mouth [aswell] : / Weigh them, it is as heavy : " These are in turn expanded into F #6's extension of Caesar's power affecting the Roman world at large ("Age, thou art sham'd . "), to be supported by F #8's "But it was fam'd with more [then] with one man?"

• In portraying himself and Brutus as nothings in comparison to Caesar, the speech opens emotionally (2/5, F #1).

• Then F #2's maxim that all men at some time are "Masters of their Fates" is cleverly extended into F #5's repeated surround phrases, suggesting equality between Brutus and Caesar—and also adding the dangerous question of how "in the names of all the Gods" has Caesar grown so powerful, all of which is strongly intellectual (14/6, the eleven and a half lines of F #2–5).

• And once the maxim is extended to judging Rome's current shame, so the intellect of the argument is pushed just as hard (14/6 in the last eleven lines of the speech), the extra breath-thoughts underscoring the smallest of points he needs Brutus to acknowledge.

- The only time anything breaks through the relentless intellectual drive is F #10's passionately ironic dismissal (2/2) of Rome being diminished: "When there is in it but one onely man".

Act II, Scene i (Brutus): Modern Text

BRUTUS It must be by his death: and for my part, 10
I know no personal cause to spurn at° him,
But for the general:° he would be crowned.
How that might change his nature, there's the question.
It is the bright day that brings forth the adder,
And that craves° wary walking. Crown him?—that;— 15
And then, I grant, we put a sting in him,
That at his will he may do danger° with.
The abuse of greatness is, when it disjoins
Remorse° from power: and, to speak truth of Caesar,
I have not known when his affections swayed° 20
More than his reason. But 'tis a common proof°
That lowliness° is young ambition's ladder,
Whereto the climber-upward turns his face;
But when he once attains the upmost round,°
He then unto the ladder turns his back, 25
Looks in the clouds, scorning the base degrees°
By which he did ascend. So Caesar may;
Then, lest he may, prevent.° And, since the quarrel
Will bear no color for the thing he is,°
Fashion it thus; that what he is, augmented, 30
Would run to these and these extremities;°
And therefore think him as a serpent's egg
Which, hatch'd, would, as his kind, grow mischievous,
And kill him in the shell.

Act II, Scene i (Brutus)

be scornful to
public (as opposed to
  "personal")

requires

harm

pity, compassion
passions ruled
truth drawn from
  ordinary experience
humility
rung
lower rungs
anticipate and thereby
  forestall
i.e., since the case against
  Caesar cannot be justi-
  fied in relation Caesar
  as he is now
extremes

10–35 Once again the play gives us a soliloquy which develops an argument. Understood in the first line is the premise that "there is no other way to accomplish unseating Caesar except by assassinating him." The rest of the speech is a series of "pros" and "cons" by means of which Brutus leads himself to justify his thesis. Here again is a speech which can be played as a stream of consciousness, a "talking aloud to oneself." The directness of the Elizabethan stage, however, gave this speech the form of a dialogue with the audience, whose thoughts and questions are silent. This must have enforced on the audience an awareness of Brutus making his tragically wrong choice of trying to achieve a good end by evil means. The choice sets in motion the events which follow—events resulting in the failure of Brutus's cause and his own destruction. With the speech given in direct address, the audience would be on the edge of saying, "No, don't do it," instead of passively listening to a stream of consciousness. At lines 14–15 is one of those small actor choices on which much thought and critical ink have been spent. Is one to suppose that "the bright day brings forth the adder and also (or therefore) requires one to walk carefully," or that "the bright day is the kind of day that brings forth the adder, and *that* kind of day requires that we walk carefully"? Perhaps the answer here can be found, as so often with these questions, by scanning the line. Have we an anapest ("and that *craves*") or an iamb ("and *that* / craves wa / ry walk / ing)? And then note the scansion of the rest of the line and what happens to the repeated "that" which changes its meaning: "*Crown / him?—that;—*" (i.e., "crown him king—imagine *that* untenable state of affairs!"). Examining such details is the actor's path toward finding the author's intended reading. The speech concludes with the "adder" image—the serpent's egg—by means of which Brutus vanquishes his own best feelings—"And to speak truth of Caesar, / I have not known when his affections swayed / More than his reason" and "since the quarrel / Will bear no color for the thing he is"—and finds justification these speculations, overriding his misgivings.

Act II, Scene i (Brutus): First Folio Speech

BRUTUS   It must be by his death : and for my part,

Background: Cassius has followed up the arguments of his speeches in Act I, Scene ii by sending Brutus several messages in different handwritings purporting to be from different concerned citizens, all urging Brutus to action, leading Brutus to explore the inevitable.

Style: Solo.

Where: The garden of Brutus's home.

To Whom: Self, and audience.

# of Lines: 25   **Probable Timing:** 1.15 minutes

Brutus

1   It must be by his death : and for my part,
    I know no personall cause, to spurne at him,
    But for the generall .

2   He would be crown'd :
    How that might change his nature, there's the question?

3   It is the bright day, that brings forth the Adder,
    And that craves warie walking : Crowne him that,
    And then I graunt we put a Sting in him,
    That at his will he may doe danger with .

4   Th'abuse of Greatnesse, is, when it dis-joynes
    Remorse from Power : And to speake truth of Caesar,
    I have not knowne, when his Affections sway'd
    More [then] his Reason .

5   But 'tis a common proofe,
    That Lowlynesse is young Ambitions Ladder,
    Whereto the Climber upward turnes his Face :
    But when he once attaines the upmost Round,
    He then unto the Ladder turnes his Backe,
    Lookes in the Clouds, scorning the base degrees
    By which he did ascend : so Caesar may ;
    Then least he may, prevent .

6   And since the Quarrell
    Will beare no colour, for the thing he is,
    Fashion it thus ; that what he is, augmented,
    Would runne to these, and these extremities :
    And therefore thinke him as a Serpents egge,
    Which hatch'd, would as his kinde grow mischievous ;
    And kill him in the shell .

Act II, Scene i (Brutus)

That Brutus is racking his brains to solve the dilemma of moving against his one-time mentor can be seen in the concentrated thought patterns F's surround phrases denote, with F's first four sentences opening with at least one, and the last two sentences ending the same way. (This is a tremendous rarity, with virtually no parallel throughout the canon.)

• The unequivocal opening " . It must be by his death : " couldn't be any bleaker, expressed as it is via a monosyllabic, unembellished surround phrase, and it seems the inevitability of Caesar's death has an emotional effect on him for the rest of F #1 (0/3).

• The same kind of bleak, unembellished surround-phrase realization opens F #2, with only the key words "nature" and "question" breaking the monosyllabic pattern: " . He would be crown'd : /How that might change his nature, there's the question ? "

• Amazingly, F #3 starts the same way, with just one very important key word, "Adder," breaking the line's monosyllabic and unembellished pattern: " . It is the bright day, that brings forth the Adder, / And that craves warie walking : "

• But the opening of F#4—" . Th'abuse of Greatnesse, is, when it disjoynes / Remorse from Power : "—though still heightened with surround phrase, now shows more release and becomes polysyllabic as more abstract fears are explored: indeed, in equating Caesar as the "Adder" and expanding on the dangerous "Sting" Caesar could now execute—though he has never yet let "his Affections" sway his "Reason"—Brutus's argument becomes highly passionate (8/7 in just seven lines to the end of F #4), as if he cannot prevent his thoughts from bursting forth.

• Yet as he finally establishes his "common proofe" focusing on "Ambitions Ladder" he becomes intellectual (5/1, F #5's first two and a half lines), only turning passionate with the corollary that the higher one climbs the more likely one is to turn his back on those below (4/4 the next three and a half lines), leading him to the firm surround-phrase understanding of what might happen to Caesar, and what he, Brutus must do about it: " : so Caesar may ; / Then least he may, prevent . "

• Which leads to great emotion (2/6, F #7) as Brutus realizes what action he must take (" ; And kill him in the shell . ") The surround-phrase strength of the conclusion is supported by the other, in part emotional, surround phrase in the sentence, thus stressing the only reason by which Caesar's death can be justified, viz.: " ; that what he is, augmented, / Would runne to these, and these extremities : "

Act II, Scene i (Brutus and Portia): Modern Text

Enter PORTIA

PORTIA   Brutus, my lord!

BRUTUS Portia, what mean you? Wherefore rise you now?
It is not for your health thus to commit°   235
Your weak condition° to the raw cold morning.

PORTIA Nor for yours neither. Y'have ungently°, Brutus,
Stole from my bed. And yesternight, at supper,
You suddenly arose, and walked about,
Musing and sighing, with your arms across;°   240
And when I asked you what the matter was,
You stared upon me with ungentle looks.
I urged you further; then you scratched your head,
And too impatiently stamped with your foot.
Yet I insisted, yet you answered not,   245
But with an angry wafter° of your hand,
Gave sign for me to leave you: so I did;
Fearing to strengthen that impatience
Which seemed too much enkindled; and withal°
Hoping it was but an effect of humor,°   250
Which sometime hath his° hour with every man.
It will not let you eat, nor talk, nor sleep;
And could it work so much upon your shape°
As it hath much prevailed on your condition,°
I should not know you Brutus.° Dear my lord,   255
Make me acquainted with your cause of grief.

BRUTUS I am not well in health, and that is all.

PORTIA Brutus is wise and, were he not in health,
He would embrace° the means to come by it.

BRUTUS Why, so I do. Good Portia, go to bed.   260

PORTIA Is Brutus sick? And is it physical°
To walk unbraced° and suck up the humors°
Of the dank morning? What, is Brutus sick,
And will he steal out of his wholesome bed
To dare the vile contagion of the night,°   265
And tempt° the rheumy and unpurgèd° air
To add unto his sickness? No, my Brutus,
You have some sick offence° within your mind,
Which by the right and virtue° of my place
I ought to know of; and, upon my knees,   270

Act II, Scene i (Brutus, Portia) 73

	233–236 Portia enters. Brutus is surprised to see her awake, and urging her "weak condition," wants her to go indoors.
	237–302 Instead of going, she presents the evidence of her own eyes that, from "yesternight at supper," he has been behaving strangely. Shakespeare was quite willing to use a device more than once if it served him, and for another scene in which another wife whose husband is involved in a conspiracy marshals evidence of his own behavior against him, the reader may refer to Lady Percy confronting Hotspur in *Henry IV Part One* Act II, Scene iii. Hotspur, too, tries to evade wifely pressure, but where that scene turns comedic, this one becomes more serious. Brutus says he is sick. Portia refutes that on the basis of his remaining in the unhealthy night air, and then demands, on the basis of their marriage vows, that by right he must confide in her. She then confronts him with her knowledge that men, masking their faces, have been to see him. He still resists. She accuses him of treating her like a harlot, not a wife. He protests that he honors her as his wife. She asserts her special strength, as wife to Brutus and daughter to Cato. Finally she cites the "voluntary wound" in her thigh. According to Plutarch, the source of this tale, she deliberately cut herself with a razor, as a result of which she came down with a fever, which could be the "weak condition" to which Brutus referred. Recovering, she used her self-inflicted wound as evidence to Brutus that she had the fortitude to keep his secret. In the play, it does seem to be the mention of the wound that moves Brutus to promise to share his troubles with her, however unclear it may be as whether he knew of it as the scene begins. For the stage the problem becomes quite practical. Does Portia merely gesture politely toward her thigh? Does she reveal her thigh wrapped with a bloody bandage? Has she just inflicted the cut and does it, unbandaged, bleed freshly? Does she show Brutus and upstage leg the audience cannot see? On the stage, the boldest choice is often the best choice, but this whole wound business is quite unpleasant for modern audiences.
expose	
constitutiton	
in a manner not befitting a gentleman	
i.e., folded across your chest (a sign of melancholy)	
waving	
besides	
product of whim	
its	
physical appearance	
disposition	
i.e., know you to be Brutus	
take, adopt	
healthful	
with doublet unbuttoned/ dampness, mist	
capacity of the night air to infect	
risk	
damp and unpurified	
harmful sickness	
power, prerogative	

I charm° you, by my once commended beauty,
By all your vows of love, and that great vow
Which did incorporate° and make us one,
That you unfold° to me, your self, your half,
Why you are heavy° —and what men tonight 275
Have had to resort to you; for here have been
Some six or seven, who did hide their faces
Even from darkness.

BRUTUS   Kneel not, gentle Portia.

PORTIA I should not need, if you were gentle Brutus. 280
Within the bond of marriage, tell me, Brutus,
Is it excepted° I should know no secrets
That appertain to you? Am I your self
But, as it were, in sort or limitation?°
To keep° with you at meals, comfort your bed,
And talk to you sometimes? Dwell I but in the suburbs° 285
Of your good pleasure? If it be no more,
Portia is Brutus' harlot, not his wife.

BRUTUS You are my true and honourable wife,
As dear to me as are the ruddy drops
That visit my sad heart 290

PORTIA If this were true, then should I know this secret.
I grant I am a woman; but withal°
A woman that Lord Brutus took to wife.
I grant I am a woman; but withal
A woman well-reputed, Cato's daughter.° 295
Think you I am no stronger than my sex,
Being so fathered and so husbanded?
Tell me your counsels,° I will not disclose 'em.
I have made strong proof° of my constancy°,
Giving myself a voluntary wound 300
Here, in the thigh: can I bear that with patience.
And not my husband's secrets?

BRUTUS   O ye gods,
Render me worthy of this noble wife!   [Knock.]
Hark, hark! one knocks: Portia, go in awhile,
And by and by thy bosom shall partake 305
The secrets of my heart.
All my engagements° I will construe° to thee,
All the character of my sad brows,°
Leave me with haste.   *Exit PORTIA*

Act II, Scene i (Brutus, Portia)

entreat earnestly, conjure

make one body of us
disclose
sad, dejected

Since Brutus seems to change because she presents her wound, the reference cannot be cut without damaging Shakespeare's structure.

303–309 What is particularly interesting here is that the significant knocking (second time for this play, and don't forget the knocking in *Macbeth*) interrupts the opportunity for Brutus to tell all, and in spite of the promise he makes to construe all his engagements, he shortly leaves with Ligarius without telling poor Portia a thing.

made an exception
conditionally or with
   restricted tenure (legal)
i.e., keep company
outskirts

at the same time
(Marcus Porcius Cato,
   Brutus's uncle as well
   as father-in-law, known
   for the strict integrity of
   his life)
secrets
test, trial   fortitude

commitments
explain in detail
what is written in
   characters on the grave
   furrows of my forehead

Act II, Scene i (Brutus and Portia): First Folio Speeches

1. PORTIA   NOR FOR YOURS NEITHER . Y'HAVE UNGENTLY
BRUTUS

2. PORTIA   BRUTUS IS WISE, AND WERE HE NOT IN HEALTH,

3. PORTIA   WITHIN THE BOND OF MARRIAGE, TELL ME BRUTUS,

Background: Already disturbed at Brutus's apparent withdrawal from their hitherto exemplary marriage of equals, and by his sudden lack of sleep and disinterest in food or her, his unwell wife Portia is further disturbed by so many men having visited him late at night, who, despite the dark, seem to have taken great pains to muffle themselves from public view. The following are her attempts to get him to share with her all his thoughts as he once did—as such each speech seems self-explanatory.

Speech #1 is her opening, triggered by his attempt to sidetrack her with "It is not for your health, thus to commit / Your weake condition, to the raw cold morning".

Speech #2 is triggered by his attempt to avoid a detailed answer to her final direct request of speech #1 with a simple "I am not well in health, and that is all".

Speech #3 is her demand for complete knowledge of what is disturbing him made full and manifest.

Style: As part of a two-handed scene.

Where: In the garden of Brutus's and Portia's home.

To Whom: Brutus.

1. # of Lines: 20   **Probable Timing:** 1.00 minutes

2. # of Lines: 20   **Probable Timing:** 1.00 minutes

3. # of Lines: 19   **Probable Timing:** 1.00 minutes

#1

Portia

1   Nor for yours neither .

2   Y'have ungently Brutus
     Stole from my bed : and yesternight at Supper
     You sodainly arose, and walk'd about,

Act II, Scene i (Brutus, Portia) 77

      Musing, and sighing, with your armes a-crosse :
      And when I ask'd you what the matter was,
      You star'd upon me, with ungentle lookes .
3   I urg'd you further, then you scratch'd your head,
      And too impatiently stampt with your foote :
      Yet I insisted, yet you answer'd not,
      But with an angry wafter of your hand
      Gave signe for me to leave you : So I did,
      Fearing to strengthen that impatience
      Which seem'd too much inkindled ; and withall,
      Hoping it was but an effect of Humor,
      Which sometime hath his houre with every man .
4   It will not let you eate, nor talke, nor sleepe ;
      And could it worke so much upon your shape,
      As it hath much prevayl'd on your {condition},
      I should not know you Brutus .
5   Deare my Lord,
      Make me acquainted with your cause of greefe .

For most of the time Portia's attempt to get a response from Brutus by simply stating the facts is handled very carefully, as the large numbers of unembellished lines show—though, as the speech develops, the imbalance of emotional releases quickly shows how difficult she is finding it to maintain self-control.

• The unembellished lines first dismiss Brutus's concerns for her health—"Nor for yours neither ."—but then swiftly turn to recalling his recent disturbing and unusual actions: "Y'have ungently . . . / Stole from my bed : and yesternight . . . / You sodainly arose, and walk'd about, / Musing, and sighing, . . . / And when I ask'd you what the matter was, / You star'd upon me,". Not only does she equally carefully describe how she pressured him for a response—"I urg'd you further, then you scratch'd your head, / And too impatiently stampt . . . / Yet I insisted, yet you answer'd not, / But with an angry wafter of your hand"—she also expresses her own responses in exactly the same way: "Fearing to strengthen that impatience / Which seem'd too much inkindled ; ". It is as if she were still taking care not to "strengthen that impatience" even now.

• The first indication of his strange behaviour is expressed via a surround phrase—" . Y'have ungently Brutus / Stole from my bed : "—while the overall summation is via an even more impassioned monosyllabic surround phrase, formed in part by the (emotional) semicolon: " . It will not let you eate, nor talke, nor sleepe ; ".

• Despite Portia's unembellished care, and the speech's intellectual opening (2/0, the first two lines of the speech), after the unembellished character (shock?) of his sudden walking about, she becomes emotional as she recalls asking "what the matter was" (0/3, F #2's last three lines).

• F #3's complete catalogue of disturbing events is still emotional, but much more carefully / only occasionally released (2/4, in nine lines).

• But then her emotion gets the better of her as she sums up the effect his actions have on both of them (F #4) and in her F #5's asking to be "acquainted with your cause of greefe" (2/7 overall in the speech's last five lines).

2 Portia

1 Brutus is wise, and were he not in health,
   He would embrace the meanes to come by it .

---

2 Is Brutus sicke?
3   And is it Physicall
   To walke unbraced, and sucke up the humours
   Of the danke Morning?
4   What, is Brutus sicke?
5 And will he steale out of his wholsome bed
   To dare the vile contagion of the Night?
   And tempt the Rhewmy, and unpurged Ayre,
   To adde unto hi{s} sicknesse?
6   No my Brutus,
   You have some sicke Offence within your minde,
   Which by the Right and Vertue of my place
   I ought to know of : And upon my knees,

Act II, Scene i (Brutus, Portia) 79

> I charme you, by my once commended Beauty,
> By all your vowes of Love, and that great Vow
> Which did incorporate and make us one,
> That you unfold to me, your selfe ; your halfe
> Why you are heavy : and what men to night
> Have had resort to you : for heere have beene
> Some sixe or seven, who did hide their faces
> Even from darknesse .

As the scene develops Portia's ability to keep herself calm begins to dissipate, as this speech clearly shows, though she does try to establish some sense of control by bringing her considerable intellect into play.

- As with the earlier speech that opens this scene (#1 above), in challenging Brutus yet again Portia opens very carefully (0/1, F #1), starting straightaway with the first of only two unembellished lines found in the speech: "Brutus is wise, and were he not in health,". This opening care is further heightened by being monosyllabic.

- Then, as she challenges his plea of sickness more directly than at any earlier time in the scene, she first becomes quite emotional (3/6, F #2–3), but finishes quite passionately (6/8, F #4–5 and the first two lines of F #6, just five and a half lines overall) as she denies his plea, finally accusing him of having "some sicke Offence within your minde".

- But, as befits the daughter of a Roman Senator famous for his skills in both debate and oratory, as she begins to demand to know "by the Right and Vertue of my place" (as Brutus's wife and partner) just what is going on, her sense of control kicks in, her intellect coming to the fore (6/2 for the next five lines).

- Sadly, this does not last, for, as she baldly states her request "That you unfold to me, your selfe", so emotions take over fully (0/6 the remaining four and half lines of the speech) and as she defines herself as "your halfe" and what she wants to know, the only two surround phrases of the speech present themselves: " ; your halfe / Why you are heavy : and what men to night / Have had resort to you : ". The first is underscored by being started via the emotional semicolon (the only one in the speech), the latter further heightened by being only the second unembellished line in the speech.

#3
Portia

1   Within the Bond of Marriage, tell me Brutus,
    Is it excepted, I should know no Secrets
    That appertaine to you?
2   Am I your Selfe,
    But as it were in sort, or limitation?
    To keepe with you at Meales, comfort your Bed,
    And talke to you sometimes?
3   Dwell I but in the Suburbs
    Of your good pleasure?
4   If it be no more,
    Portia is Brutus Harlot, not his Wife .

---

5   I graunt I am a Woman ; but withall,
    A Woman that Lord Brutus tooke to Wife :
    I graunt I am a Woman ; but withall,
    A Woman well reputed : Cato's Daughter .
6   Thinke you, I am no stronger [then] my Sex
    Being so Father'd, and so Husbanded?
7   Tell me your Counsels, I will not disclose 'em :
    I have made strong proofe of my Constancie,
    Giving my selfe a voluntary wound
    Heere, in the Thigh : Can I beare that with patience,
    And not my Husbands Secrets?

F's three separate slight onrushes (F #2, #5, and #7) show where, despite her intellect and logic, Portia's control slips, as do the three extra breath-thoughts found in the first four lines of the speech. And though F #5 is formed of five consecutive surround phrases, underscoring the strength of her determination, the fact that four of the five are in part formed by the (only) two emotional semicolons in the speech it seems that even here she has to struggle not to let her emotions get the better of her.

Act II, Scene i (Brutus, Portia)

- The speech's opening argument based on the "Bond of Marriage" is strongly intellectual (4/1, F #1), though it seems Brutus's lack of reply breaks this pattern, for the next question (whether she plays only a limited role in his life) is highly passionate (3/4, the three lines of F #2)—but this break is only momentary, for, despite the very strong imagery that follows, starting with a long (thirteen-syllable line) and ending with her suggestion she is merely his "Harlot, not his Wife", she manages to reestablish intellectual control (4/0, F #3–4).

- And it seems his lack of reply causes this pattern to break yet again, for the demanding and repetitive five consecutive surround-phrase sequence forming F #5 swings back to intellectual passion yet again (9/5 in just four lines).

- Though F #6's direct challenge as to her worth ("no stronger than my Sex") swings back to intellectual control (3/1), the demand seems a little difficult for her, for two extra breath-thoughts split the two-line sentence into four thoughts rather than the two in most modern texts.

- And the intellectual strength of F #7's surround phrases opening—" . Tell me your Counsels, I will not disclose 'em : " (0/1)—and the speech's final challenge—" . Can I beare that with patience, / And not my Husbands Secrets ? " (3/1)—only serve to illustrate how hard she is still trying to maintain self-control, even though the "strong proofe of my Constancie" is offered passionately yet again (2/3).

Act III, Scene ii: Modern Text

ANTONY Friends, Romans, countrymen, lend me your ears;
I come to bury Caesar, not to praise him. 70
The evil that men do lives after them,
The good is oft interrèd with their bones;
So let it be with Caesar. The noble Brutus
Hath told you Caesar was ambitious.
If it were so, it was a grievous fault, 75
And grievously hath Caesar answered it.°
Here, under leave of Brutus and the rest—
For Brutus is an honorable man;
So are they all, all honorable men—
Come I to speak in Caesar's funeral. 80
He was my friend, faithful and just to me:
But Brutus says he was ambitious;
And Brutus is an honorable man.
He hath brought many captives home to Rome
Whose ransoms did the general coffers° fill. 85
Did this in Caesar seem ambitious?
When that the poor have cried, Caesar hath wept.
Ambition should be made of sterner stuff,
Yet Brutus says he was ambitious;
And Brutus is an honorable man. 90
You all did see that on the Lupercal°
I thrice presented him a kingly crown,
Which he did thrice refuse. Was this ambition?
Yet Brutus says he was ambitious;
And, sure, he is an honorable man. 95
I speak not to disprove what Brutus spoke,
But here I am to speak what I do know.
You all did love him once, not without cause;
What cause withholds you then, to mourn for him?
O judgment! thou art fled to brutish beasts, 100
And men have lost their reason. Bear with me;
My heart is in the coffin there with Caesar,
And I must pause till it come back to me.

If you have tears, prepare to shed them now.
You all do know this mantle.° I remember 165
The first time ever Caesar put it on;

Act III, Scene ii (Antony)　　　　　　　　　　　　　　　　　　　　83

69–80 Antony has some trouble getting their attention, and once he does, he is careful to disclaim undue affection for Caesar—only to "bury," not to "praise." He quickly stresses that he speaks "under leave of Brutus and the rest" and uses the word "honorable" in all earnestness, both of Brutus and the other "honorable men." A performance note: As Antony begins to speak and all through his oration, the crowd responds, both as indicated by the author's written lines for the Plebeians and at other places the cast and director find appropriate. No actor can outshout an unrestrained crowd, and many an Antony, trying to do so on the first day of rehearsal, has developed vocal strain that has stayed with him through the run. While retaining a feeling of spontaneity rising to hysteria, the crowd must be so precisely rehearsed that they are never actually speaking at the same time as Antony.

paid the penalty for it

public treasury

81–95 "He was my friend, faithful and just to me," Antony begins to build his picture of Caesar. The captives and their ransoms, his pity for the poor, his denial of the crown on the Lupercal—these are Antony's building blocks, and after each he reiterates that Brutus is honorable but says Caesar was ambitious. The actor need not invoke irony yet, as he speaks of Brutus. He is simply demonstrating contradictions and asking his audience to think.

on the day of the Lupercalia

96–99 Antony here seems to lose his earnest self-control and bursts out with passionate honesty and a plea for their respect and decency. His audience apparently stands shocked into silence.

100–103 He stares at them, appalled by their lack of "reason," and then craves their indulgence, overcome by emotion. As he controls his weeping and "recovers," he gives the onstage audience a chance to digest his words.

cloak (the Roman toga)

164–192 His first line ("If you have tears . . .") is just a simple statement, or warning. As he reminds the

'Twas on a summer's evening in his tent,
That day he overcame the Nervii.°
Look, in this place ran Cassius' dagger through:
See what a rent the envious° Casca made: 170
Through this the well-belovèd Brutus stabbed;
And as he plucked his cursèd steel away,
Mark how the blood of Caesar followed it,
As rushing out of doors, to be resolved°
If Brutus so unkindly° knocked,° or no; 175
For Brutus, as you know, was Caesar's angel.°
Judge, O you gods, how dearly Caesar loved him.
This was the most unkindest° cut of all;
For when the noble Caesar saw him stab,
Ingratitude, more strong than traitors' arms, 180
Quite vanquished him. Then burst his mighty heart;
And in his mantle muffling up his face,
Even at the base° of Pompey's statue,
Which all the while ran blood,° great Caesar fell.
O, what a fall was there, my countrymen! 185
Then I, and you, and all of us fell down,
Whilst bloody treason flourished° over us.
O now you weep, and I perceive you feel
The dint° of pity. These are gracious° drops.
Kind souls, what° weep you when you but behold 190
Our Caesar's vesture° wounded? Look you here,
Here is himself, marred° as you see, with° traitors.

Act III, Scene ii (Antony)

a fierce Gallic tribe
   conquered by Caesar
   in 57 B.C.
malicious

learn for certain
unnaturally and cruelly
rapped on a door /
   delivered a powerful
   blow
dearest friend, darling
most unnatural and cruel

pedestal
(according to popular
   belief, the corpse of a
   murdered man bleeds
   in the presence of his
   murderer)
swaggered

force   full of grace, virtuous
why
garment
mangled, ruined   by

crowd of the mantle, our audience should remember that some of the onstage audience would have been veterans of Caesar's wars, and everyone there would have seen Caesar, in parades or triumphs, probably wearing this very mantle. In the Elizabethan costume of Shakespeare's own period, it was certainly logical that the cloak we saw Caesar don on his way to the Capitol would have been a cloak he might have worn a day of battle. When the production elects to use Roman costume with actors in ceremonial togas, this sequence loses in logic. The usual solution, if Roman costume is wanted, is to have Caesar put on the red Imperial toga, not really in use till a later day, which looks at least somewhat military. A duplicate version, with appropriate rents and stains, over a duplicate bloodstained tunic, is then put on the "corpse" for the oration, and Antony beside the body, demonstrates as the text indicates. The entire section seems to require great simplicity and tenderness of the actor, not releasing his passion until line 187—"Whilst bloody treason flourished over us." People in the crowd are by now weeping openly, on which he comments, and then, in lines 191–192, he really lets go, as he violently pulls the mantle away: "Look you here, / Here is himself, marred as you see with traitors."

Act III, Scene ii: First Folio Speeches

1. Antony   Friends, Romans, Countrymen, lend me your ears :

2. Antony   If you have teares, prepare to shed them now .

Background: Unwisely as it proves, Brutus, over Cassius's objections, has given Antony permission not only to participate in the funeral orations for Caesar, but to present Caesar's body to the general populace too. Young though he may be, and despite his protestations of being a poor orator ("I am no Orator, as Brutus is ; / But . . . a plaine blunt man"), he succeeds in turning the people against the conspirators. The following are just two examples from the longer scene: speech #1 is the famous opening; speech #2 prepares the people for the sight of Caesar's mutilated body.

Style: Public, open-air address in front of a large group.

Where: The steps of the Capitol.

To Whom: The common people.

1. # of Lines: 35   **Probable Timing:** 1.45 minutes

2. # of Lines: 29   **Probable Timing:** 1.30 minutes

#1

Antony

1   Friends, Romans, Countrymen, lend me your ears :
     I come to bury Caesar, not to praise him :
     The evill that men do, lives after them,
     The good is oft entterred with their bones,
     So let it be with Caesar .

2   The Noble Brutus,
     Hath told you Caesar was Ambitious :
     If it were so, it was a greevous Fault,
     And greevously hath Caesar answer'd it .

3   Heere, under leave of Brutus, and the rest
     (For Brutus is an Honourable man,

Act III, Scene ii (Antony)   87

     So are they all ; all Honourable men)
     Come I to speake in Caesars Funerall .
4   He was my Friend, faithfull, and just to me ;
     But Brutus sayes, he was Ambitious,
     And Brutus is an Honourable man .
5   He hath brought many Captives home to Rome,
     Whose Ransomes, did the generall Coffers fill :
     Did this in Caesar seeme Ambitious?
6   When that the poore have cry'de, Caesar hath wept :
     Ambition should be made of sterner stuffe,
     Yet Brutus sayes, he was Ambitious :
     And Brutus is an Honourable man .

7   You all did see, that on the Lupercall,
     I thrice presented him a Kingly Crowne,
     Which he did thrice refuse .
8   Was this Ambition?
9   Yet Brutus sayes, he was Ambitious :
     And sure he is an Honourable man .
10 I speake not to disproove what Brutus spoke,
     But heere I am, to speake what I do know ;
     You all did love him once, not without cause,
     What cause with-holds you then, to mourne for him?
11 O Judgement! thou [are] fled to brutish Beasts,
     And Men have lost their Reason .
12   Beare with me,
     My heart is in the Coffin there with Caesar,
     And I must pawse, till it come backe to me .

Two questions often raised are "Just how politically shrewd is Antony?" and "How deliberate and preplanned is his manipulation of the crowd?" In this speech, F's orthography suggests that while the argument Antony wishes to make is probably predetermined, at times personal emotion seems to break through—though whether the end of the speech is pre-planned or a genuine moment of loss of control is up to each actor to decide.

- While most of the surround phrases seem to underscore a specific point Antony wishes to drive into the Crowd's collective consciousness, the two that start the speech—" . Friends, Romans, Countrymen, lend me your ears : / I come to bury Caesar, not to praise him : "—seem to be necessary simply to quieten down the crowd, while the only two formed in part by emotional semicolons—" ; all Honourable men) / Come I to speake in Caesars Funerall . /He was my Friend, faithfull, and just to me ; "—seem to reflect Antony's difficulty in handling the death of Caesar rather than designed to advance any particular argument (though whether this is a public ploy to gain sympathy or genuine pain is up to each actor to decide).

- Most of the remaining surround phrases hammer away at the two themes Antony keeps returning to, Brutus being (by implication not really) "Noble" and Caesar being (by implication not really) "Ambitious":

> " . The Noble Brutus, / Hath told you Caesar was Ambitious : "
> " : Did this in Caesar seeme Ambitious ? / When that the poore have cry'de, Caesar hath wept : "
> " : And Brutus is an Honourable man . "
> " . Yet Brutus sayes, he was Ambitious : / And sure he is an Honourable man . "

The last in the speech presents the key concept by which he hopes to sway the crowd:

> " . O Judgement ! thou [are] fled to brutish Beasts, / And Men have lost their Reason . "

- The opening to quieten the crowd and set up the theme of "Noble Brutus / Caesar... Ambitious" starts intellectually (8/2, F #1 and the first line and a half of F #2), while the suggestion that if Caesar was ambitious he has "greevously... answer'd it" and the explanation that he, Antony, is speaking now with the permission of the "Honourable men" is very passionate (8/7 in the six lines made up of the last two lines of F #2 and all of F #3).

- As Antony begins to put forward the clever juxtaposition of Brutus saying Caesar was Ambitious with the direct evidence (the "Ransomes" of "Captives" used to fill the "generall Coffers") that Caesar was anything

Act III, Scene ii (Antony) 89

but, he manages to keep much of his feelings in check (11/5, the six lines of F #4–5), though the two-line direct reference to Caesar's response to the crying poor, that ambition should be made of "sterner stuffe", becomes highly emotional for just a moment (1/3, the first two lines of F #6).

• Returning to the theme of the "Honourable Brutus" saying Caesar "was Ambitious" and then clearly demonstrating that Caesar was not, Antony gets his emotions back under control once more (11/6, the last two lines of F #6 through to F #9—seven lines in all), the intellect heightened by the demanding (and tactic-revealing) three word F #8: "Was this Ambition?"

• Whether Antony is making another public ploy to gain sympathy or is genuinely upset, the last three sentences show no consistency. F #10's suggestion / question "What cause with-holds you then, to mourne for him?" is highly emotional (1/5); the short statement that "Judgement" is now lost is highly intellectual (4/1, F #11); and the final admission "My heart is in the Coffin there with Caesar" (2/3, F #12) is passionate.

#2

Antony

1   If you have teares, prepare to shed them now .

2   You all do know this Mantle, I remember
    The first time ever Caesar put it on,
    'Twas on a Summers Evening in his Tent,
    That day he overcame the [Nervy] .

3   Looke, in this place ran Cassius Dagger through :
    See what a rent the envious [Caska] made :
    Through this, the wel-beloved Brutus stabb'd,
    And as he pluck'd his cursed Steele away :
    Marke how the blood of Caesar followed it,
    As rushing out of doores, to be resolv'd
    If Brutus so unkindely knock'd, or no :
    For Brutus, as you know, was Caesars Angel .

4   Judge, O you Gods, how deerely Caesar lov'd him :
    This was the most unkindest cut of all .

5   For when the Noble Caesar saw him stab,

>   Ingratitude, more strong [then] Traitors armes,
>   Quite vanquish'd him : then burst his Mighty heart,
>   And in his Mantle, muffling up his face,
>   Even at the Base of Pompeyes Statue
>   (Which all the while ran blood) great Caesar fell .
> 6 O what a fall was there, my Countrymen?
> 7 Then I, and you, and all of us fell downe,
>   Whil'st bloody Treason flourish'd over us .
> 8 O now you weepe, and I perceive you feele
>   The dint of pitty : These are gracious droppes .
> 9 Kinde Soules, what weepe you, when you but behold
>   Our Caesars Vesture wounded?
> 10   Looke you heere,
>   Heere is Himselfe, marr'd as you see with Traitors .

Whatever personal emotion Antony was undergoing during the opening of the scene in the previous speech, here F's orthography suggests that Antony has a much better grip on himself, with just four extra breath-thoughts, especially the ones relating to the stab wounds (the "rents") in Caesar's cloak (the "mantle"), in F #3 and F #5 suggesting moments where his personal feelings might just break through without the tiniest need for self-control.

• The fact that F #1 is emotional is beyond doubt (0/1), though whether this is genuine or a ploy is again up to each actor to decide.

• In displaying the highly emotionally charged, blood-stained cloak of Caesar and the first rents the conspirators' daggers made, the slightly onrushed F #2 (split into two by most modern texts) is totally factual (6/0, F#2, and 3/1, F #3's, first two lines)—though how Antony knows which rent was made by which conspirator is highly suspect since he was drawn away from the actual murder by Trebonius as part of the conspirators' plans: nevertheless, the stakes are even further increased with the description of these first rents being set as surround phrases.

• But as Antony turns to the rent supposedly made by Brutus, his passions come to the fore (4/4, F #3's next five lines), and then, whether deliberate or not, he intellectually intensifies the attack on Brutus via the three surround phrases: " : For Brutus, as you know, was Caesars Angel . /

Judge, O you Gods, how deerely Caesar lov'd him : / This was the most unkindest cut of all . " The last line is heightened by being unembellished, as if the quietness of the utterance were all that was needed to move the crowd.

- And having (presumably) hushed the crowd, Antony's intellect kicks in as he first describes this as the blow that "burst his Mighty heart" (F #5), going on (F #6–7) to superbly manipulatively reason that "Then I, and you, and all of us fell downe" (11/3 overall).

- And then the emotional F #8 recognition (1/4) of having worked the crowd to where he wants them is highlighted by being set as two surround phrases (" . O now you weepe, and I perceive you feele / The dint of pitty : These are gracious droppes .") . . .

- . . . while the final revelation of the body itself is (triumphantly? personally distressingly?) passionate (5/7, the last three lines of F #9–10).

www.ingramcontent.com/pod-product-compliance
Lightning Source LLC
Chambersburg PA
CBHW080553170426
43195CB00016B/2775